HORRIBLE HISTORIES

SLIMY STUARTS

TERRY DEARY

ILLUSTRATED BY **MARTIN BROWN**

■SCHOLASTIC

For Fiona and Vanessa King – much nicer Kings than the historical ones

Scholastic Children's Books,
Euston House, 24 Eversholt Street,
London, NW1 1DB, UK

A division of Scholastic Ltd
London ~ New York ~ Toronto ~ Sydney ~ Auckland
Mexico City ~ New Delhi ~ Hong Kong

First published in the UK by Scholastic Ltd, 1996
This edition published 2007

Some of the material in this book has previously been published in
Horrible Histories The Massive Millennium Quiz Book/Horribly Huge Quiz Book

Text copyright © Terry Deary, 1996, 1999
Illustrations © Martin Brown, 1996, 1999
All rights reserved

10 digit ISBN 1 407 10429 2
13 digit ISBN 978 1407 10429 4

Printed and bound by CPI Group (UK) Ltd, Croydon, CRO 4YY

14

CONTENTS

Introduction

History can be simply horrible. This history book is simply horribly *interesting*. It will tell you things about Stuart times that not many teachers know.

James I used the power of the rack to torture Guy Fawkes. Now you can torture your teacher with … the power of *the question!*

You can amaze your relations with terribly true tales of dreadful deeds…

Become the most popular person in your class by learning new words. Yes, even *you* can become the *dossy* with a little practice.

You'll end up knowing a bit more about life in the slimy 17th century. The funny, the foul and the fantastic. They are all here...

Slimy Stuart timeline

1603 Elizabeth I kicks the royal bucket. Last of the Tudors. James VI of Scotland comes down to be James I of England as well. First of the Stuarts.

> *Slimy Jim, snotty Jim,*
> *Slobbered when he drank*
> *his beer;*
> *Hated witches, hated ciggies.*
> *Loved to murder little deer.*

1605 A plot to blow James all the way back to Scotland is discovered – known as the Gunpowder Plot. Guy Fawkes gets the blame.

1616 Playwright, William Shakespeare, dies on his 52nd birthday. That probably spoiled the party a bit.

1621 Puritans who can't stand James settle in America. They don't bother to ask the native American Indians, of course.

1625 James I turns up his regal toes – he snuffs it. Son Charles I gets to put bum on throne.

> *Charlie One, on the run;*
> *He'd upset the Roundhead chaps.*
> *Said that God was on his side;*
> *God not there when Charlie axed!*

7

1629 Charles upsets Parliament in a row over who's in charge, them or him. Slimy Charlie says he can rule without them. And, to prove it, he does.

1637 Charles upsets the Scots by trying to force them to use his new Prayer Book. Charles has the nerve to call Parliament again to help him. Charlie and Parli just argue.

1642 War breaks out between Charlie (with his Cavaliers) and Parli (with their Roundheads). Brother fights brother.

1647 Charlie loses war and makes friends with the Scots and with Parliament. Sadly, Parliament is now ruled by its army under General Oliver Cromwell who makes sure…

1649 Charlie gets the chop. Royal head in un-royal bucket. England ruled without a king until…

1658 Oliver Cromwell dies and his son Richard takes over until …

1660 The 'Restoration' – the monarchy returns with Charles II. Cromwell dug up, strung up and beheaded – *very* slimy.

Charlie two used to woo
Lots of women, what a bloke!
Merry monarch – plague then fire,
Sent the laughter up in smoke.

1665 The Great Plague – in London alone 100,000 people die … and just as many rats.

1666 The Great Fire of London – destroys many of the filthy wooden buildings that housed the plague.

1685 King Charles II sick. Given 'Spirit of Human Skull' but dies anyway. (He apologized to his doctors for taking so long to die.) Catholic brother, James II, takes over.

King Jim, rather dim;
Made it clear he liked the Pope.
Britons told him,
'Push off, Jimmy!
Catholic Britain? Not a hope.'

1688 James thrown off throne. Even his daughter, Mary, is glad to see the back of him. She takes over with hubby, William of Orange.

Mary big, ate like pig;
Willie small like her pet eat.
Smallpox killed her; as for Willie,
His horse stumbled, he went splatt!

9

1702 Mary's sister, Anne takes over the throne – she doesn't share it with hubby. When you're as fat as Anne there's no room to share a throne with a pin.

> *Annie, stout; feet with gout;*
> *Food and brandy she would gorge.*
> *Children all dead, no more Stuarts;*
> *Throne passed on to German George.*

1707 England and Scotland united under one Parliament.

1714 Anne pops her clogs – just as her 17 children have before her. End of slimy Stuarts.

Slimy James I (reigned 1603-1625)

The Stuarts were a funny lot … funny-'peculiar'. *Not* so funny-'haha' if you were one of their victims. They were wheelers and dealers, always ducking and diving to keep out of trouble. You could never be quite sure what they were up to. In fact they were rather slimy characters. The slimy Stuarts.

James the slob

James was 37 when he became king of England. He had a straggling brown beard and hair, watery blue eyes and spindly legs. A French visitor described James when he was 18 years old…

He was of middle height, more fat because of his clothes than his body. His clothes always being made large and easy, the doublets quilted to be dagger-proof. His breeches were in great pleats and full stuffed. He was naturally timid, his eyes large and always rolling after any stranger came into his presence. His beard was very thin. His tongue too large for his mouth which made him drink very badly as if eating his drink which came out into the cup from each side of his mouth. His skin was soft because he never washed his hands, only rubbed his finger ends slightly with the wet end of a napkin.

And those were just his good points! Fontenay forgot to mention James was bow-legged and picked his nose. The king used his sleeve instead of a handkerchief ... though he sometimes preferred to use a finger and thumb. Maybe Fontenay didn't notice! Among James's other bad habits were swearing and drinking too much.

A famous historian called Macaulay said James was like *two* men. One was a witty scholar who argued well – the other was a 'nervous drivelling idiot'. You decide which from something that happened when he arrived in England. James complained that the people of England were forever pestering him to make a public appearance. He refused – very rudely.

"BUT YOUR MAJESTY, THEY ONLY WANT TO LOOK UPON YOUR FACE"

"ZOUNDS! WHY DON'T I PULL MY BREECHES DOWN AND THEY CAN LOOK UPON MY BACKSIDE?"

A wit? Or a twit?

Killer James

James I wasn't so sure of English customs when he arrived from Scotland. On his way to be crowned in London he stopped at the town of Newark. As the crowds packed the streets to greet him a pickpocket was caught. James ordered that the pickpocket should be hanged. The obedient councillors had the man executed.

Only *then* did they quietly tell James that in England the king did not have the power to put anyone to death without trial. This was no comfort at all to the pickpocket.

On his way to London James enjoyed some hunting. To make sure the king had enough fun the English cheated. They kept hares in cages and let them out in time for the king to catch them.

Gunpowder, treason … and lies?

Everybody knows about Guy Fawkes … or do they? Test your teacher with these well known 'facts' about Guy Fawkes and the Gunpowder Plot. How many are true and how many false?

1 Guy Fawkes was born a Catholic.
2 Guy Fawkes was the leader of the gunpowder plot.
3 Luckily, Guy Fawkes was caught just before he blew up James and his Parliament.
4 Guy Fawkes was tortured and betrayed his friends.
5 Guy Fawkes was burned on a bonfire.

Answers: False! False! False! False! Oh, and … false!

13

Here's how…

1 Guy (or Guido as he was christened) was brought up a Protestant. When he was ten his new stepfather (Denis Bainbridge) taught him to follow the Catholic religion. The Catholics had already tried to dispose of Elizabeth I (with a little help from foreign friends, Armadas and poisonous plots). James was just another Protestant monarch to be disposed of … nothing personal!

2 The leader of the Gunpowder Plot was Robert Catesby. Guy was fighting as a soldier for the Spanish army when the plot was first dreamt up. He was smuggled back into England to help – probably because he was an explosives expert.

THIS IS A BOMB

GOSH!

3 Guy was caught at least 12 hours before Parliament was due to meet the king. And it wasn't 'luck'. The soldiers who caught Guy had been tipped off and were searching for explosives when they found him there. King James had also been tipped off. He was never in any real danger from the Gunpowder Plot.

4 Guy was tortured on the rack for two days before he even gave his real name. It took another two days before he confessed to the plot then *six* more days before he named any other plotters. But, by that time, his partners had already been hunted and arrested or killed. They *had* been betrayed … but not by Guy Fawkes.

5 Guy was due to be hanged, drawn and quartered. This was the punishment for 'treason', a crime against the king. Burning was for a crime against the Church.

Slimy James

Not everybody loved James when he arrived. What James needed was to give the English a shock. He needed to say, 'You'd be worse off if I was dead!' … then arrange an attempt on his own life. A *failed* attempt, naturally. Is that what this slimy Stuart did?

1 First find an enemy who would want James dead. The Catholics were a good choice.

2 Get spies to persuade a Catholic group to kill the king – suggest a plot to blow him up in Parliament with all his ministers.

3 Then catch them just in time.

On November 5th 1605 the king's chief minister, Robert Cecil, said…

It has pleased God to uncover a plot to kill the King, Queen, Prince and the most important men of this land, by secretly putting gunpowder into a cellar under Parliament and blowing them all up at once.

Guy Fawkes, who was caught in the cellars of the Houses of Parliament, was tortured and executed.

As an example to others, an execution for treason was super-savagely slimy. After hanging the victim for a few moments he was cut down and cut open. His guts were thrown on to a fire before he was beheaded and cut into quarters.

Guy cheated the executioner, who wanted Guy to really suffer. When the rope was placed round Guy's neck he jumped off the ladder so that his neck broke. He was dead when they cut him open – and the executioner was dead disappointed.

The English people were so shocked at the thought of losing their new king that James became more popular than ever … and the Catholics more hated and feared. Or was that what James wanted? A Catholic visitor to England in 1605 said…

Some people are sure that this was a trap. The government tricked these men.

So, did slimy James 'set up' Guy Fawkes to be caught?

Did you know?
James spent a lot of money on rich clothes, but he had no use for the magnificent jewelled dresses of Queen Elizabeth I. The Master of the Wardrobe sold over 1,000 of them and made himself a fortune!

Curious cures

Stuart medicine was a mixture of the clever and the crazy. *Clever* William Harvey discovered that blood 'circulates' – that is to say it goes from the heart, round the body, back to the heart and off again. Harvey discovered this by cutting up corpses, of course. He was so used to dead bodies that he wasn't bothered when he saw so many victims after the battle of Edgehill. In fact he sat under a hedge and read a book to pass the time. Then he grew cold … so he pulled a corpse over him to keep warm.

Before Harvey's discovery people knew that blood moved, but they thought it went backwards and forwards like a Yo-Yo. At the same time some *crazy* doctors still believed that a good way of curing someone was to let a lot of that blood out of the body. They tried this for almost every illness known.

Similarly, people couldn't agree about the effects of smoking. Most people know about James I's hatred of smoking. He said smoking was…

… a custom loathsome to the eye, hateful to the nose, harmful to the brain, dangerous to the lungs, and in the black stinking fumes it resembles the smoke of the pit that is bottomless [Hell].

James then put large taxes on tobacco to put people off smoking. *Clever* James I. But, while the king was writing those wise words, the smokers were pointing to crazy Nicholas Culpeper's *Complete Herbal* book of 1653, where he claimed that tobacco...

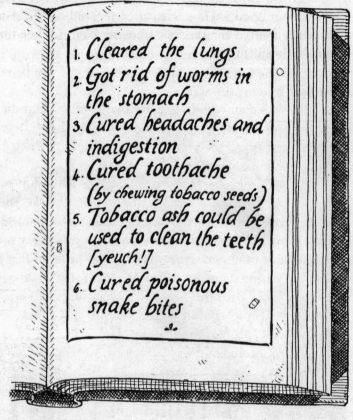

1. Cleared the lungs
2. Got rid of worms in the stomach
3. Cured headaches and indigestion
4. Cured toothache (by chewing tobacco seeds)
5. Tobacco ash could be used to clean the teeth [yeuch!]
6. Cured poisonous snake bites

He also claimed that rubbing tobacco juice into children's heads would kill lice in their hair.

Who would you rather believe? King James or Nicholas Culpeper?

Did you know?

Sir Walter Raleigh was said to have brought tobacco to Britain. In 1994, anti-smoking campaigners said Raleigh was to blame for 300 deaths a week from smoking illnesses. Queen Elizabeth II was asked to take Sir Walter's knighthood from him – even though he'd been dead nearly 400 years. The Queen refused, saying, 'He suffered enough.' That was true. James I cured Sir Walter's smoking habit for good by having his head cut off.

A sick idea

Smallpox was a common disease in Stuart times. Many died from it – 1,500 smallpox deaths in London in 1659. If you recovered from the disease then your face would probably be scarred for life with marks left by the spots.

Children recovered better than adults. So what would you do if you heard someone nearby had smallpox? Take your child to visit them in the hope that the child would catch the disease! They were probably young enough to recover and could go through life without having to worry about it.

Find the cure! Here are ten illnesses. If you were a Stuart doctor what would you prescribe? Match the cure to the illness … just don't expect them to work and *don't* try them on your friends!

Illness   I

1 Accidentally swallowing a snake (!) [Boot it out]
2 Heavy bleeding [This should make it all write]
3 Stopping yourself from becoming drunk [Make a pig of yourself]
4 Colic (stomach pains) [The cure shouldn't kill you stone dead]
5 Toothache [You'll be oak-kay after this]
6 Consumption (lung disease) [This should slip down nicely]
7 Fever [Coo—what a thought]
8 Accidentally swallowing a horse leech in drinking water [Make it flee]
9 Preventing the plague from infecting you [A rich food]
10 Jaundice (liver disease) [wear a clothes peg on your nose]

Cure

a *Place a cold marble stone (on which the sun has never shone) on the stomach*

b *Drink a mixture of fleas and vinegar*

c *Eat snails boiled in milk and a few chopped worms if you wish*

d *Burn the sole of an old shoe and breath in the smoke*

e *Place a gold coin in the mouth*

f *Write the word 'Veronica' on your left thumb*

g *Take two 'tench' fish, split them open and place them on the feet. Leave for 12 hours 'even if they begin to stink,' then put fresh ones on*

h *Cut a pigeon in half and place one half on each foot*

i *Scratch your gum with a new nail then drive the nail into an oak tree*

j *Eat the roasted lungs of a pig first thing in the morning*

Answers:

1 d) *R. Surflet, 1600.* He reckoned snakes could creep into farmers' mouths as they slept in the fields. He also swore the cure was 'tried and approved'.

2 f) *Madam Suzannah Avery, 1688.* She actually wrote a book with many sensible cures in. This wasn't one of them.

3 j) *John Goldsmith, 1678.* Other medicines included powdered berries of ivy dissolved in vinegar. After that you probably couldn't face drinking anything else!

4 a) *Traditional cure.* Probably helped soothe the pain! If you couldn't find a piece of marble then a lump of turf was supposed to work too. (If you want to try this, shake the worms out first.)

5 i) *J. Aubrey 1670.* He said, 'This cured William Neal's son when he was so mad with pain he was ready to shoot himself.'

6 c) *Traditional cure.* Stupid Stuarts? Well, this cure was made even slimier by the American settlers who brought it from Britain – they ate a *live* snail every morning for 9 days. And they were still doing it in 1929!

7 h) *Traditional cure.* No good for the fever sufferer. Worse for the pigeon!

8 b) *R. Surflet, 1600.* If you accidentally swallow a horse leech while drinking a glass of water it's probably your eyes that need seeing to!

9 e) *John Allin, 1665.* Doctor Allin said a coin with Queen Elizabeth's head on works best.

10 g) *J. Aubrey, 1670.* Don't *eat* the used fish – bury them or the cure won't work.

Charles I (reigned 1625-1649)

Ch-ch-ch-charlie

Charles I didn't really expect to be king. His older brother, Henry, was the first in line to the throne. But Henry fell ill. Doctors suggested a remedy of pigeons pecking at the bottom of his feet! Henry died – Charles was heir to the throne.

Charles was shy and nervous but tried hard to cover this up by acting strong. He had his father's Scottish accent and a squeaky little voice with a stammer. His eyes never rested on the people he was talking to, but seemed to look through them. Charles had few friends. He listened to his father's favourite adviser, Buckingham, and really let him run the country. But Buckingham was stabbed to death by a soldier. The soldier was upset because Buckingham hadn't given him the promotion he thought he deserted.

Charles's fatal friends

When Buckingham was murdered Charles grew closer to his wife, Henrietta Maria. The British people thought this was dangerous because she was a Catholic and they never really trusted her or liked her.

Charles also asked Thomas Wentworth, nicknamed 'Black Tom', for advice. Black Tom was hated for his brutal methods.

Charles's Archbishop of Canterbury, William Laud, gave Charles bad advice as well. Laud angered the Scots *and* the

Puritans with his orders ... he wanted them to pray just like those dreaded Catholics! The Puritans entered Parliament and tried to bring in new laws.

Parliament raised an army ... so Charles raised an army. The King's army (the Royalists or Cavaliers) fought the army of Parliament (the Roundheads).

Slimiest acts

Slimy act 1: Parliament wanted Charlie's best pal, Black Tom, executed. Charles said he'd protect Black Tom within a week of making that promise he signed Black Tom's death warrant.

Slimy act 2: When Charles started to lose the Civil War he made a secret deal with the Scots. They would send an army to help him. The Roundhead leader, Cromwell, was furious! He said this was treason to the English people ... and the punishment for treason should be death!

24

Charlie was one slimy Stuart who tried to be slimy once too often. He lost the war and Parliament sent him to be executed. That put a stop to his slimy games.

The execution of Charles

Charles stepped on to the scaffold and prepared to say those famous last words … but what were they?

As he took off his jewels and handed them to the bishop beside him he said, 'Remember!' Brilliant! What a dramatic last word! But, no. Charlie had to go and spoil it.

After a few moments of silent prayer he took off the cloak and put his neck on the block. The executioner brushed Charles's hair to the side to give him a clean cut.

Charles said, 'Wait for the sign.' *What a let-down.* 'Wait for the sign.' What sort of last words are they? They could be the last words of a policeman trying to stop a steam-roller at a crossroads.

Anyway, Charles stretched out an arm, the axe fell and severed the head cleanly. The crowd surged forward and some dipped handkerchiefs in the blood.

Did you know…?

After his execution Charles's head was sewn back on to *his* body so relatives could pay their last respects before he was buried. After Cromwell's death, however, his body was dug up and hanged, then thrown in a ditch!

Slimy Stuart riddle

The Scots hated Charles I's *Church of England Prayer Book* – but Scottish priests were ordered to use it. One Scottish bishop only dared to read it to his angry congregation if he held a loaded pistol in each hand. The Scots didn't want to be Church of England – they wanted to be *Presbyterians*.

Test your teacher with this old riddle: Presbyterians are said to be the most religious people. Why? (Clue: rearrange the letters of 'Presbyterians' to make a phrase of three words with four, two and seven letters.)

Answer: 'Best in prayers'.

The Civil War

A 'civil' war is where people in one country fight among themselves. They are usually especially slimy affairs. The English Civil War was no different. It had its fair share of comical and gruesome moments…

1 In The English Civil War (1642-1649), brother fought brother and sometimes groups of soldiers switched sides. Sir Faithful Fortescue's men changed sides – but they forgot to change the sashes they wore when fighting … so their new allies shot them!

2 Sir Arthur Aston was not a nice man. When one of his soldiers committed a crime he ordered that the man's hand should be sawn off. But a year later Sir Arthur was showing off on his horse to impress some ladies. He fell off and broke his leg. It turned septic … and had to be sawn off.

3 But that wasn't the end of Sir Arthur's punishment for his cruelty. He had a wooden leg fitted and boasted he was as good a fighter as any man with two legs. He wasn't. In 1649 his army was defeated by Cromwell at Drogheda in Ireland. A soldier caught Sir Arthur and beat his brains out. What did the soldier use to batter him? Sir Arthur's own wooden leg, of course.

4 Prince Rupert, the Royalist leader, took his white poodle, Boy, with him everywhere – including to his battles. The Roundheads were afraid of the dog's devilish powers. They said Boy could talk several languages and make himself invisible. They thought he also gave his master the power to be weapon-proof. Then, at the battle of Marston Moor, Boy wandered on to the battlefield and was killed.

5 King Charles's army suffered from having some dimwitted generals. In 1644 Lord Byron took charge of some fresh troops from Ireland and surrounded the Roundhead town of Nantwich. No Roundhead could get out of the town because Lord Byron's troops made a circle right round Nantwich even though the town was on the edge of a river! It was icy weather. The river was frozen. Brilliant Byron's troops could cross it when they liked. Surely Nantwich would surrender? But … *the ice melted*. The troops across the river were cut off, and Byron's two half-armies were easily defeated. Just to make things worse, bird-brain Byron's fed-up Irish troops agreed to switch sides and fight with the Roundheads.

6 Lord Byron managed to do even *worse* at the next battle – Marston Moor, in Yorkshire. He sat with his horse-soldiers (cavalry) behind a deep ditch and rows of foot-soldiers with pikes. All he had to do was wait for the order and attack the Roundheads. Then he saw the Roundheads coming towards him. They would be slowed up by the ditch and battered by the pike men.

All he had to do was *wait*. He couldn't. He charged forward. First he *flattened* his own pike soldiers, then he got his own men tangled in their own ditches where the Roundheads were able to cut them to pieces. The battle was lost and with it the whole of northern England. All because Lord Byron couldn't wait.

7 The Cavalier leader, Prince Rupert, also came face to face with the Roundheads on Marston Moor, in 1644. By the time he reached the battlefield there was just an hour of daylight left. Hardly worth starting a battle now, he thought. So he ordered his men to stop and have supper. The Roundheads couldn't believe what they were seeing. While the Cavaliers were having a bite to eat the Roundheads attacked and massacred 3,000 of them. They fought on in the moonlight and by midnight the Cavaliers had lost the battle.

8 In 1643 a group of London women surrounded the Houses of Parliament shouting, 'Peace and the King.' They were asked to leave. They refused and started beating up Members of Parliament – especially the crop-haired Puritans. In the end the army was called in to drive them out. Three women were killed and many others locked in prison.

9 The Cavalier town of Colchester, Essex, was under siege in 1648. The siege went on for three months and the inhabitants were forced to eat cats and dogs. It got worse. When they heard that Cromwell was winning the war, they gave up. The leaders expected to be treated honourably as prisoners of war. The Roundheads took them to Colchester Castle and shot them. (Maybe they were cat-lovers.)

ANOTHER TIDDLES ON TOAST DEAR?

10 The Parliament forces had problems too. Beeston Castle was left in the care of a Parliament commander whose peace-time work was selling cheese. One night a Cavalier officer and eight men climbed the rock that the castle was built upon and crept into the castle. The cheese-seller was so shocked he surrendered his 60 men … and then invited the attackers to supper and a drink of beer. When the angry Roundheads caught up with the cowardly cheese-seller, they shot him.

The spooky Stuarts

The stuffed chicken's revenge

Francis Bacon was a great statesman in the days of James I. (No jokes about his name, please.)

WE'RE HAVING BACON FOR DINNER TONIGHT

STRANGE, MOST PEOPLE HAVE BACON FOR BREAKFAST

Then he got involved in a scandal and had to give up government work. Instead he turned his great brain to solving the problems of the world. (Sir Francis was an expert on manure, among other things.)

The problem of preserving food was one that strained his brain for a while. Then, as he was riding through London one snowy March day, he noticed that the frozen grass in the tracks was as fresh as ever. 'Aha!' he thought. 'Maybe the cold is preserving the grass. I wonder if it would preserve meat the same way?'

He ordered the coachman to stop the carriage at the nearest farm. He jumped out and bought a chicken. The coachman was ordered to kill the chicken, to pluck out most of its feathers and to clean out its insides. This he did.

Sir Francis bent down and began stuffing the chicken full of snow. He then packed it into a sack full of it.

But the cold was too much for 65-year-old Francis. He started shivering and collapsed in the snow. Within a few days he was as dead as the chicken.

Deader than the chicken, in fact. For the chicken wasn't

finished. It continues to haunt the place to this day. Half-stripped, it runs and flaps and shivers around Pond Square in London. Someone tried to catch it during World War Two but it disappeared into a brick wall. It was last reported in the 1970s. But that's not the only Stuart ghost story...

The Civil War soldier spooks

One of the Civil War battles was at Edgehill on October 23rd 1642. Charles claimed that he'd won – so did Cromwell!

Charles's nephew, Prince Rupert, led a charge of horse soldiers. It was a great success. They broke through the Roundhead lines and reached their supply wagons. But the nutty nephew didn't know what to do next. The Cavaliers spent some time plundering the supplies then decided to join the battle again. Unfortunately they were too late. Charles was already running away to Oxford.

Two months later some farm workers near Edgehill complained that they were disturbed at night by the charging of horses, the roar of cannon and the blowing of bugles. The villagers went to see what was happening ... and they saw the battle of Edgehill – again. And again. And again ... and again. Ghosts seemed to be acting out the battle every weekend.

Charles sent some of his officers to report and they saw the battle too. Charles's reporters had been at the original battle and recognized some of the ghostly soldiers. They saw Sir Edmund Verney who had been holding the king's flag until his hand was cut off – still holding the flagpole.

The ghostly battle can still be seen every year on October 23rd, it is said...

Chopped Charlie's last chance

Charles himself was visited by a ghost…

The terror of Tedworth

One of Britain's most famous ghost stories happened in Stuart times. It concerns the *Phantom Drummer of Tedworth*.

Magistrate John Mompasson was visiting the town of Ludgershall in Wiltshire when he heard the deafening sound of a drum.

'What's that horrible racket?' he asked.

It's a beggar. He has a special licence to beg and to use that drum to attract attention,' his friend explained.

'Look, I know the magistrates round here. None of them would sign a licence like that. Fetch him here.'

So the beggar, William Drury, was brought before Mompasson and showed his licence. It was a very clumsy forgery. Drury went to prison but begged to be allowed to keep the drum. Mompasson refused. Drury escaped from the prison and the drum was sent to Mompasson's house.

For the next two years the house suffered terrible drumming noises. Then the ghost grew more violent...

- A bible was burnt.
- An unseen creature gnawed at the walls like a giant rat, purred like a cat and panted like a dog.
- Coins in a man's pocket turned black.
- Great staring eyes appeared in the darkness.
- The spirit attacked the local blacksmith with a pair of tongs

- A horse died of terror in its stable.
- Chamberpots were emptied into the children's beds.

I DIDN'T WET THE BED MUM, HONEST!

Drury was arrested again for stealing a pig in Gloucester. He claimed it was his witch powers that were cursing Mompasson. So Drury was tried for witchcraft and sentenced to transportation overseas.

The haunting of Mompasson's house stopped. Drummer Drury was lucky. Twenty years earlier he would have been burnt at the stake as a witch.

Test your teacher

Is your teacher a historical brainbox or a hysterical bonehead? Test him/her/it with these simple true or false questions…

True or false?

1 In 1648 James II was a 14-year-old prince. His father had lost the Civil War and the young prince had to escape from England. To disguise himself he dressed as a servant with old clothes and a dirtied face.

2 Roundheads were called Roundheads because of the shape of their helmets.

3 Cavalier General, Prince Rupert, taught his dog to cock its leg every time someone said the name of the Roundhead leader, 'Pym'.

YOU SHOULD SEE WHAT HE DOES IF SOMEONE SAYS 'CROMWELL'

4 Charles I went to France to marry Henrietta.

5 The Earl of Berkshire committed suicide by shooting himself with a bow and arrow.

6 At some cattle markets men sold their wives.

7 Stuart boys wore petticoats until they were six years old.

8 In south-west England children were forbidden to smoke.

9 People believed that a dead person's tooth, worn as a necklace, prevented toothache.

10 Guy Fawkes was arrested and taken to King James's bedroom to be questioned.

Answers:

1 False. James dressed as a girl with a specially made dress. The tailor who made the dress was given James's measurements. He said he'd never known a woman that shape before – but he made it anyway and it fitted. Anne Murray, who helped him, said 'he looked very pretty in it.'

2 False. It was the shape of their crop-haired heads that gave them their name. In fact many Cavalier soldiers wore the same helmets as the Roundheads and became so confused at times that they killed their own allies.

3 True. It also jumped happily in the air when he said 'Charles'.

4 False. He didn't go *anywhere* to marry her. He sent his friend, the Duke of Buckingham, who acted as Charlie's stand-in at the wedding in Notre Dame, France.

5 False. The Earl of Berkshire *did* commit suicide but he used a cross-bow and bolt. Easier than a longbow, but equally horrible.

6 True. This did happen from time to time. One husband was so pleased with the five guineas he got for his wife that he went to Stowmarket and ordered the church bells to be rung.

7 True. At the age of six they were 'breeched' – given their first pair of trousers – in a ceremony. They were also given a small sword to wear.

8 False. Children in Somerset, Devon and Cornwall actually took their clay pipes to school. Smoking was

considered healthy then. Pupils at Eton were ordered to smoke during the plague years because it was said to help you avoid the disease. The smell could well have sent the plague-rats packing.

9 True. Some people went into graveyards to dig skeletons up and pinch their teeth.

10 True. Knowing some of James's disgusting personal habits, a visit to his bedroom could have been nastier than a visit to the torture rack.

Teach your teacher ... Silly Stuart facts.

Impress your teacher and get a wonderful report at the end of term. How? Approach teacher's chair/desk/cage and say 'I was reading a jolly good history book the other day and I learned some amazing facts...' then amaze/ entertain/ sicken your teacher with these intriguing tales. (One each day for a week should do the trick).

• Here's a sad thing ... Off the coast of Cornwall is the dangerous Eddystone Rock. In 1693 Henry Winstanley built a lighthouse to warn ships away. The 26-candle lighthouse was built of rock and stone. Iron bars were sunk into the rock to keep it as firm as the Eddystone Rock itself. In 1703 a storm swept the lighthouse away. Winstanley may have been disappointed for a short while - a *very* short while. He was inside it at the time and disappeared with his invention.

• Here's a weird thing ... The people of Caernarvon in Wales were desperate for a ferry boat to carry them across their river. They were so desperate that they pinched the wood from Llanddwyn church to build the boat. 'God will be angry,' the villagers of Llanddwyn said. 'So what?' the boat-builders replied. So … the ferry sank in 1664 and 79 people drowned. 'Told you so,' taunted the villagers of Llanddwyn.

• Here's a curious thing … Some Stuart tramps made money by performing marriage ceremonies for couples. They called themselves Strollers' Priests. The marriage was made by the bride and groom shaking hands over the corpse of a dead horse.

HE'S NOT DEAD YET, BUT HE HASN'T GOT LONG TO GO

These marriages were not legal, of course.

• Here's a nasty thing … During the Civil War the soldiers used simple muskets – pour the powder down the barrel, put the lead shot in, light the powder: 'Bang!' Or, sometimes, 'Bang … ouch!' Because accidents were common. As one Royalist officer said, 'We bury more toes and fingers than we do men.'

• Here's a horribly historical thing … An essential substance in gunpowder was 'saltpetre'. This was made from bird-droppings and human urine. Government officers had the right to dig these ingredients from hen-houses and toilet. In 1638 'saltpetre men' tried to get permission to go into churches to collect material because, 'women pee in their seats which causes excellent saltpetre.' (It must have been those long, long, sermons!)

Remember, remember…

Remember, remember the 30th of January! Charles I is remembered by some Church of England churches which have been named after him. Charles is remembered as a martyr who died for his religion. Charles churches can be found in Tunbridge Wells, Falmouth and Plymouth.

Remember, remember the 29th of May! It used to be Oak Apple Day and celebrations were held in remembrance of the Royal Oak … the tree that Charles II hid in to save his life. Oak Apple Day is now generally forgotten, but many towns now have a pub named after the Royal Oak – perhaps your town has.

Remember, remember the 3rd of September! On that day a small group of Oliver Cromwell supporters gather outside the Houses of Parliament. They sing a few hymns and a bugler plays a military tune of farewell, The Last Post. This marks the day of Cromwell's greatest victories (at Dunbar in 1650 and Worcester in 1651). It was also the day on which Cromwell died.

Remember, remember the 5th of November! James made this a public holiday when Guy Fawkes failed to blow up Parliament – 'Fawkes was the only man to enter the Houses of Parliament with an honest reason,' some people have said! But in 1678 there was a fear of another Catholic plot, so on November 5th people burned images of the Pope.

Sickly Stuart snacks

Would you like to have eaten like a Stuart? Like the Tudors before them, the rich people ate a lot of meat. They had servants to do the hard work of preparing it. Turning meat over an open fire was a hard job. It was usually given to a young kitchen boy whose front would be roasted by the fire, while his back would be chilled by the draught of the cool air drawn into the flames.

So the inventors of Stuart times came up with a couple of clever devices. One was a clockwork turner. The other was a sort of large 'hamster-wheel'. But instead of a hamster you popped a dog inside. As the dog walked forward, the meat turned.

The people of Stuart times not only invented new ways of cooking. They also discovered new food ideas…

The inventive Stuarts

Which of the following new food fads became popular in Stuart Britain?

Answers:

1 Yes. A Chinese legend says that Emperor Shennong learned how to make tea in 2737 BC when a few leaves from a tea plant accidentally fell into water he was boiling. A likely story. But it wasn't until the Stuart age that tea-drinking became popular in Britain. People of the 17th century thought it was quite all right to drink tea from the saucer. It took another 300 years (1920 to be exact) for someone to invent tea bags.

2 No. British politician John Montagu, fourth Earl of Sandwich (1718-1792), had a habit of eating beef between slices of toast so he could play cards without stopping to eat. But he was born *after* the Stuarts. And, though he gave his name to that type of food, the idea of eating meat between bread was first tried by the Romans over 1,000 years before.

3 No. Blame the Tudors for that. Sir Anthony Ashley of Dorset brought cabbages to Britain from Holland. (The stewed green mush you get for school dinners is not quite that old. Honest.)

4 Yes. Forks had been used on royal tables as early as the 14th century but only became popular when Thomas Coryat published a book about their use in Italy. Most people in Britain had used knives with sharp points to 'spear' their food and had spoons to scoop up the smaller pieces.

5 Yes. Oliver Cromwell was presented with a pineapple in 1657. The first in Britain. He probably didn't know whether to eat it, wear it or give it a bowl of milk.

6 Yes. Coffee was a popular Arab drink for hundreds of years before the Stuarts discovered it in the middle of the 17th Century.

7 Yes. From the early 1660s 'ice houses' with thatched roofs were built, or snow pits were dug in the ground. Winter snows were kept all year round. Sweet cream (sometimes with orange-flavoured water) was frozen for a couple of hours and then served.

THE RECIPE SAID MIX ORANGE AND CREAM THEN STAND IN ICE HOUSE FOR TWO HOURS

8 Yes. Thomas Johnson showed bananas in his London shop window in 1633.

9 Yes. The Spanish brought chocolate back from Mexico in 1519. But it became really popular in Stuart Britain. In the 17th century, 'chocolate houses' were the popular meeting places of the day, rather like the local pub today. But you probably wouldn't have enjoyed the drink; it was full of cocoa butter and rather greasy. Some dealers added soil to the cocoa paste to cheat the buyers.

10 No. The Dutch first made eating chocolate in 1828.

Eat like a Stuart

If you were invited to eat at an upper-class house then you'd eat off fine silver and gold plates … but you'd be expected to take your own spoon. Forks were not generally used until the reign of William and Mary at the end of the Stuart age.

Then Stuart people discovered how *really* useful forks could be. They found they were great for picking out bits of food that got stuck between your teeth!

And that wasn't their only habit that we'd find a bit disgusting today. They used their fingers a lot to pick up meat – and threw the bones on the floor for the dog. Everyone at the table used the same bowl to rinse their fingers in – and some people even rinsed their spoons in the same water.

One writer described a gentleman's country house in Dorset…

A house so badly kept that it shamed him and his dirty shoes. The great hall was scattered with marrow bones, it was full of hawks' perches, hounds, spaniels and terriers. The upper sides of the hall were hung with fox skins from this year's and last year's skinning. Here and there a polecat intermixed. Usually two of the great chairs in the parlour had litters of cats on them and the gentleman always had two or three accompanying him at the dinner table.

But some people worried about good table manners. A Stuart book gave advice on how to eat politely. Its top ten recommendations were…

If you wish to be POLITE at the DINNER TABLE

· Wipe not your greasy fingers upon the tablecloth
· Dip your food into the common salt dish before you eat it but not after you have taken a bite from it
· Bring not your cat to the dinner table
· Pick not your teeth with your fingers or your knife
· Make not a noise as you drink your soup
· Shout not at the table, 'I eat none of this, I eat none of that etc.'
· Blow not upon your soup to cool it
· Belch not at the table
· Spit not and cough not at the table
· Scratch not your head whilst you sit at the table

Fair gingerbread

People enjoyed going to fairs and eating. They didn't have candy-floss and hot dogs, though. Their favourite fair food was gingerbread. Some of the towns, like Birmingham, had Gingerbread Fairs. Want to know what gingerbread tasted like in Stuart times? Try this recipe.

Stuart Gingerbread

Ingredients
225g white breadcrumbs
5ml ground ginger
5ml cinnamon
5ml aniseed
25g sugar
150ml water

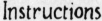

Instructions
1 Dry the breadcrumbs in an oven but don't let them turn brown
2 Mix the other ingredients in a saucepan and add the dried breadcrumbs
3 Warm gently and blend with a wooden spoon until you have a stiff dough
4 Dust a chopping board with ground ginger and cinnamon
5 Turn the dough out onto the board and roll it to about 5mm thickness
6 Cut into small circles (about 2-3 cm across)
Eat them without further cooking

Have a cup of tea (sugar but no milk) with your gingerbread for a truly Stuart snack. And, talking about eating…

Stuart food you may not want try

Stuart Christmas Pudding

Do you like Christmas Pudding? Most people do. You probably enjoy the candied peel, raisins, sugar and spices. So did the Stuarts. They were all in the Stuart pudding ... along with *chopped cow's tongue and chicken*. Fancy a spoonful?

Sweets

Decorate your table for that special occasion with sugar models. Make them into the shapes of animals and plants. Eat them to finish off the meal. Sir Hugh Platt described how to make the stuff in 1609:

> *Take violets and heat them with a little hard sugar. Steep them in rosewater and grind them into a paste. This will have the colour of the violet and smell of the violet. In the same way you may work with marigolds, cowslips, primroses or any other flower.*

Eating flowers! Whatever next? Carnations and custard? Pansy pie? Baked buttercups and tulips on toast?

Charles II (reigned 1660-1685)

Cheerful Charlie

The leader of the Roundheads, Cromwell, died in 1658. His son wasn't very keen on running the country and the British people wanted a king again. So Charles I's son, Charles II, returned to the throne.

Charles II was known as the Merry Monarch because he brought back all the games and entertainments the Puritans had banned.

He wisely agreed to work along with Parliament in future. But Members of Parliament were still worried about a Catholic take-over – Charles was married to Catherine of Breganza, a Catholic princess from Portugal! Still, Charles himself was a good Protestant … wasn't he?

Slimiest act

Parliament wanted to pass a law which banned any Catholic from ever becoming king - this was aimed at Charles's younger brother, James, who was a Catholic. Charles II was annoyed and sent Parliament away so the law couldn't be passed. He ruled without Parliament until his death in 1685 … then James came to the throne as the royal family had planned.

But, slimiest of all, Charles II knew he couldn't be King of England *and* a Catholic - so he *pretended* to be a Protestant. Then, as he was dying, he told a Catholic priest he wanted to die a Catholic. He was 'converted' on his death-bed.

Charlie's cheerless childhood

In 1641 Charles I was forced to sign the death warrant for his friend, the Earl of Strafford. He wondered if Parliament might like to change its mind so he sent his son Charles to ask if they'd like to change Strafford's sentence to life imprisonment ... or, if they *had* to execute him, could they at least wait until Saturday, please?

Young Charles toddled off to Parliament with his dad's message ... he was just ten years old. The prince soon learned what a tough life it was. Parliament refused the plea and executed Strafford the next day.

Within a year little Charlie was involved in the Civil War and trying to take on a fully armed Roundhead with his pistol at the battle of Edgehill. He shouted 'I fear them not!' as the Roundhead charged ... but a Cavalier arrived just in time to save his royal bacon.

The Great Escape

In 1651, when Charles II was a prince, he was at the Battle of Worcester, fighting against the Roundheads. His army lost. He fled to a friendly house and was hunted by the Roundheads. Charles's friend, Colonel Carlis, led him to a huge oak tree. They climbed into it and the house owner took the ladder away. The king managed to sleep in the tree with a pillow he'd taken.

With the help of a haircut and a face blackened by soot, Charles escaped to Holland and safety.

Fire and plague

Londoners who lived through Charles II's reign were pretty lucky … lucky that the plague didn't get them! And if the plague spared their lives then the Great Fire probably destroyed their houses. Would *you* have survived in Stuart London?

The plague … read all about it!

with the others and went off to the graveyard'.

His partner, Chris Cross (24-ish) added, 'We was just about to unload the cart when the bodies started moving, didn't they? Gave me a right turn, I can tell you. Turned out to be this singer trying to get out of the cart. What a mess. Bodies all over the place!'

Smelly

Wandering minstrel Elwiss Prestley, of no fixed abode, said 'I'd had a few jars of ale and just sat down for a nap. Woke up under this fat, smelly feller. Thought it was somebody trying to muscle in on my sleeping spot. Told him to get off, didn't I? Course he didn't reply … well, he wouldn't, him being dead like.'

Tonic

Sam and Chris were able to laugh about their grave mistake. 'We'll buy Elwiss a drink to make up for it,' Sam said. 'We can afford it – after all, business is good at the moment. They're dropping like flies.' Asked how he stays so fit and healthy Chris said he put it all down to 'Doctor Kurleus's Cureall Tonic'.

Doctor Kurleus Cures All

This is to give notice that John Kurleus, former physician to Charles I, offers a drink and pill that cures all sores, scabs, itch, scurfs, scurvies, leprosies and plagues be they ever so bad. There is no smoking or sweating or use of mercury or other dangerous and deadly substances. Doctor Kurleus sells the drink at three shillings to the quart and the pill one shilling a box. He lives at the Glass Lantern Tavern, Plough Yard in Grays Inn Lane

He gives his opinion for nothing

Plague pottiness

Doctors *said* that dogs and cats, pigs, pet rabbits and pigeons could spread the plague. The government believed them and tried to prevent the plague by killing all the dogs in the town. Dogs were banned from towns and dog-killers were appointed to round up strays.

Other doctors blamed dirty air – huge bonfires were lit in the hope that they would 'purify' it.

No one understood that the real enemy was the rats, whose fleas spread the plague. That fact wasn't discovered until 1898.

Other doctors offered miracle cures for the plague. They would also offer free treatment, as in the advert (above). There was a catch, of course. Doctor Kurleus would look at a plague victim and say, 'You need a quart of my medicine. That'll be three shillings please.'

'I thought your advert said you give your opinion for nothing!'

'I do,' the devious doctor would shrug. 'My *opinion* is free, the *drink* is three shillings.'

Sick people, afraid of dying a painful plague death, would give anything for a cure. The fake doctors grew rich and the people died anyway.

Dying to get to heaven

When there was no plague and families had time to bury their dead properly, the people of Stuart times had some curious customs. You may have thought burying corpses with money and belongings went out of fashion when Tutankhamun died. It didn't.

A 17th-century body was buried with…
• a coin (to pay St Peter at the gates of heaven)
• a candle (to light the way to heaven)
• a 10-centimetre layer of bran cereal on the bottom of the coffin (for comfort).

There was also a custom in some counties for families to hire a 'sin-eater'. This was a poor person who was given a loaf of bread to eat and a beer to drink …

while standing over the corpse. The idea was the dead person's dead sins would enter the bread and be eaten – their ghost could then get into heaven.

Graves should have a headstone with a rhyme carved on to it. For example…

HERE LIES THE CARCASS
OF HONEST JOHN PARKHURST

Awful rhyme – but difficult with some surnames. What would you rhyme with your name?

Fire from France
This is the story usually told about the fire…

1 A little boy crept into Thomas Farriner's baker's shop in Pudding Lane. He reached up to steal a loaf that was cooling by the window. The baker swung round quickly. Too quickly – he scattered ashes over the wooden floor.

OI! WHAT YOU UP TO!

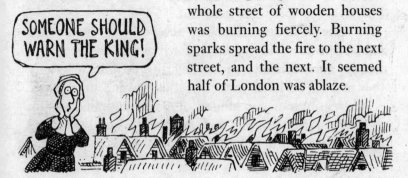

SOMEONE SHOULD WARN THE KING!

2 The shop caught fire. Soon the whole street of wooden houses was burning fiercely. Burning sparks spread the fire to the next street, and the next. It seemed half of London was ablaze.

3 When Charles heard of the problem he did two things…

> MY ORDERS ARE TO BLOW UP HOUSES TO STOP THE SPREAD OF THE FIRE

> YAY!

4 And then the King himself set off to join the fire-fighters. He ended up blackened by smoke and soaked with water ... but won huge popularity with the people of London.

5 So did his final action…

> YAY!

> AND HERE IS A PURSE OF 100 GUINEAS FOR THE BRAVE FIRE-FIGHTERS!

That's the *heroic* story. Teachers never tell you the horrible historical *truth*. Did you know, for example, the people of London blamed French spies for starting the fire? Whenever they met a Frenchman in the street they would attack him.

A blacksmith met an innocent Frenchman walking down the street and struck him with an iron bar 'until the blood flowed in a plentiful stream down to his ankles.'

A crowd threw a French painter's furniture into the street then ripped his house to the ground. 'Maybe you'd like to set fire to it,' they said, 'just like you set fire to the rest of London!'

Several innocent foreigners were dragged in front of magistrates and charged with starting the fire. Then the son of a French watchmaker *confessed!* No one knows why. Farriner the baker (where the fire had started) said the watchmaker could not have got into the bakery to start the fire.

What did the magistrate do with this unfortunate Frenchman?

1 Deported him back to France.

2 Put him in jail so the mob couldn't take their revenge on him.

3 Set him free.

4 Hanged him anyway, if that's what he wanted!

James II (reigned 1685-1688)

Dim Jim

Charles II died without children so the crown passed to his brother, James II. But James was a *Catholic* and the people of Britain still had that fear and hatred of Catholics. The only thing that saved him was the fact that he had no son to take over after his death.

His daughter, Mary, was a good Protestant and husband William was the Dutch Protestant leader. When James died, Protestant Mary would lead the country. Things were fine ... until a 'son' suddenly and mysteriously appeared! Was this another slimy, sneaky Stuart plot?

THE KING'S HAD A BOY!

THAT'S VERY SUSPICIOUS. MEN SHOULDN'T BE HAVING BABIES

Slimiest act - the warming-pan switch

James's wife, Mary of Modena, had five babies from 1672 till 1682 – and they all died. Then she was expecting another baby. When it arrived her doctor was miles away. Two nurses saw to the birth. To the horror of the British people it was a living boy! It would become another Catholic king! But a story went around...

- The two nurses had been paid the huge sum of £500 each – to keep them quiet?

- Mary's baby had died – but someone else's new-born baby boy was smuggled into the Queen's room!

- The baby was smuggled into the room in a warming-pan – a metal pan with a lid, usually filled with coals and used to warm a bed.

- The Queen's dead baby was smuggled out in the same pan.

Jamie's judge

Four months after James came to the throne there was a rebellion led by the Duke of Monmouth. The duke's rebel force was smashed at Sedgemoor, in Somerset, by James's troops. Monmouth was executed.

That wasn't good enough for James. He had all of Monmouth's supporters rounded up as well and sent to trial. He wanted revenge. He wanted to destroy, wipe out, annihilate, eradicate, exterminate, obliterate and mangle all opposition. He couldn't do that himself. He had to have some sort of trial – and some judge who would be as ruthless and rotten as necessary.

He chose Judge George Jeffreys. Good choice. He was described by the writer Violet Van Der Elst as follows…

Judge Jeffreys was known to have a very handsome face and at times would look almost kind and angelic. But there was no man living who had a blacker soul. Innocent men were hanged along with the guilty. There was the case of Charles Lindell. He said he had not left his shop – in fact he was arrested there. The night he was supposed to be out fighting with Monmouth he was sitting at home with his mother and sweetheart. All this he told to Judge Jeffreys. With his most kindly smile he listened and seemed to sympathize. Then his face twisted into a most horrible grimace as he turned to the poor prisoner, who had thought he had a good hearted judge. He now realized the judge was a fend, not a man. Judge Jeffreys told him he would be hanged by the neck, if not for taking part in the rebellion then for telling lies under oath. This man was only one of nearly two hundred that Judge

Jeffreys condemned to death Another eight hundred were sentenced to transportation and slavery in the colonies – a slower but equally certain form of death.

WE'RE HEADING FOR A FATE WORSE THAN DEATH

WHAT'S THAT?

AMERICA

The trials were known as 'The Bloody Assizes' - no prizes for guessing why. The angelic judge did have a little soft spot for Lady Alice Lisle – he actually let her sit down during her trial because she was 70 years old. She was accused of sheltering rebels. She was found guilty and the thoughtful judge sentenced her to be burnt.

The executed rebels had their bodies preserved in tar. The bodies were then sent around the west of England as a warning to anyone else who thought of rebelling.

BUT, there was some Stuart justice … after James II was finally overthrown in December 1688, Jeffreys was arrested; he died in the Tower of London.

Cowardy custard James

But did Dim Jim really expect to get away with the warming-pan trick? If he did then he was disappointed. Another Catholic king was more than the British could bear. They didn't wait for the baby to grow up and take over the throne.

Parliament invited Dim Jim's daughter, Mary, to take the throne with her very Protestant husband, William.

William landed in England – James ran off to Ireland. William's take-over was known as 'The Glorious Revolution'.

In 1690 James II tried to defend Ireland against William. He lost the Battle of the Boyne and retreated safely to Dublin. He met Lady Tyrconnel, an Irish noblewoman, in Dublin and complained...

Jim slipped away to France and safety.

Jim the brave

James wasn't afraid of fighting once he got into a battle. At the Battle of Lowestoft – a sea battle against the Dutch – he spent 18 hours on deck while sailors all around were being shot down. As the famous poet *didn't* say...

> *The king stood on the burning deck*
> *Till all the Dutch were beat,*
> *The crown of England on his head...*
> *And blisters on his feet*

64

Slimy Stuart crime

The Stuart age was one of the classic ages of the highwayman. Stage–coach journeys had begun. 'Stand and deliver! was the famous cry and the horse ride from London to York was the amazing achievement of one man … but which one?

The great escape

But what was the great adventurer's name?
1 Dick Turnip (nicknamed Tricky Dicky)
2 William Nevison (nicknamed Swift Nicks)
3 Dick Turpin (nicknamed Dick Turpin)

You've probably heard the famous story about Dick Turpin riding from York to London to avoid being convicted of a robbery. Turpin *never made that ride*. A writer simply pinched the Nevison story and tacked it on to the Turpin tale.

Nevison met King Charles II, who gave him the nickname and a pardon. The Merry Monarch had a habit of doing that – even when the crime was one of the greatest in history…

Blood and the Jewels

Some people become famous because of what they do. And some become famous because of what is done to them. Talbot Edwards had that sort of fame. He lived to a good old age but never grew tired of telling people about the time he was robbed…

Old Talbot Edwards sat in the corner of the tavern and emptied his mug of ale. He ran a tongue over his toothless gums and enjoyed the flavour. Then he pushed the mug across the table to the young couple who sat opposite him. 'Another pint of ale will help my memory,' he smiled.

The young man signalled and the landlord brought a fresh jug to the table. Talbot dabbed at his watery eyes with a grubby handkerchief and reached for the ale. 'So you've heard about me, eh?'

'We have, Mr Edwards,' the young man said eagerly. 'I'm writing the story for a newspaper and wanted to hear your side of it.'.

'It's ten years since the robbery,' Talbot shrugged. 'Why now?'

'Because Blood's dead,' the young woman put in.

The old man blinked and paused with his mug half way to his lips. 'Blood? Dead? No-o. Blood's not the sort of man to die. I just don't believe it.' He shook his head slowly.

'Tell me about him,' the young man urged.

Talbot Edwards sat back on the oak bench and half closed his eyes. 'Funny little feller, Colonel Blood. Ugly face with smallpox scars, short legs and brilliant blue eyes. Lovely Irish voice. He could talk the tail off a pig. I was in charge of the Tower of London back in 1671 when he turned up on my doorstep. He was dressed like a parson, and he *told* me

68

he was a parson … so I believed him!'

'He was a soldier, though, wasn't he?' the young woman asked. 'Came to England to fight for Cromwell and the Roundheads?'

Old Talbot threw back his head and laughed. 'Bless you, no! He came to England to fight for the Cavaliers … he only switched sides to the Roundheads when he realized that King Charles was going to lose!' He chuckled and supped his beer. 'Of course he wasn't too popular when Charles the Second came back to the throne. The new government took everything Tom Blood had.'

'That's when he decided on the robbery?' the reporter asked.

'Aye. But being Colonel Blood it couldn't be any ordinary robbery, could it? No. It had to be the most daring robbery of all time. He had to go for the Crown Jewels, didn't he.'

'And it was your job to guard them?' the young woman asked.

'I was the keeper. Lived on the floor above the jewel room. Of course, my job was to show visitors the jewels – especially *respectable* visitors like 'Parson' Blood. And I never suspected a thing. He spent months setting it up, you

69

see. Brought his wife with him on the second visit.

I remember she took ill in the jewel room and my wife Nell looked after her. Parson Blood was so grateful he came back two days later with a pair of new gloves for Nell. After that he became a sort of friend of the family.'

'And he didn't show an unusual interest in the jewels?'

'No–o. He seemed more interested in making a match between his rich nephew and my daughter. Of course the women were keen on that!' old Talbot said.

'So how did the robbery happen?' the reporter asked.

'I'm coming to that,' the old man said and took a long drink of his ale. 'Parson Blood brought his good-looking nephew to meet Nell and Alice – that's my daughter – and he brought a couple of friends along too. "Now we don't want to be bothered with this marriage business, Talbot, do we?" Blood says. "No," I says. "Why don't we take my two friends here down for a look at the jewels while the women have a chat?" And I agreed.'

'And that's when he tried to steal the jewels?' the young woman asked.

'I'm coming to that,' Talbot Edwards said. 'Being a private visit I didn't have any of the Tower guards around, did I? So, there I was, alone in the jewel room with three villains. No sooner had I unlocked the door than Blood gave me a whack over the head with a wooden mallet. When I woke up they'd already pulled away the iron grating and were pulling out the crown, the sceptre and the orb A hundred thousand pounds' worth of jewels … what a robbery, what a man!'

'You sound as if you admired him,' the puzzled young woman said.

Old Talbot chuckled. 'Can't help it, can't help it. Anyway, when I woke up I found they'd tied my hands and feet. I started shouting, "Treason! Murder!" That's when Blood drew his sword and ran it through my shoulder ... lucky it missed my heart, really. Want to see the scar?' he asked and reached for the buttons on his doublet.

'No!' the young woman said quickly and turned up her small nose with a little show of disgust.

Talbot Edwards shrugged. 'That's when Blood had his one stroke of really bad luck. Like I said, it was a private visit so we shouldn't have been interrupted. They'd flattened the crown with the mallet and were stowing the jewels in a bag. Who should arrive at the Tower? My own son. On leave from the army fighting in Holland. I wasn't expecting him – and Blood certainly wasn't. He made a run for it with his nephew and his two helpers. The blood was pouring out of my chest but I managed to shout out. My son heard and came and found me.'

The old man was becoming excited now and his watery eyes were glowing in the yellow light of the candles.

'Your son raised the alarm?'

'He did. A sentry tried to stop Blood . . . so Blood shot him. The second sentry saw that and ducked. He let the robbers through the first door. There was a lot of confusion, you understand – guards were attacking each other by mistake. That let Blood reach his horse at the gate. But the Captain of the guard, a man called Beckman, saw what was happening and grabbed Blood just before he got on his horse. Blood pulled out a pistol, pulled the trigger . . . and had his second bit of bad luck. The pistol misfired. Beckman wrestled him to the ground and the whole gang were arrested.'

The young woman leaned forward. 'What I don't understand is why didn't Blood hang for the crime?'

The old keeper shook his head. 'Didn't I tell you? Blood could charm milk from a bull. He insisted he had to talk to King Charles himself. In the end the king agreed to see him. Now, Blood knew the king liked an adventurous rogue. Sure enough, Charles pardoned him . . . even gave him lands in Ireland worth £500 a year to make up for what he'd lost.'

'And the king gave *you* a reward,' the reporter said.

The old man looked into his empty ale mug a little shyly. 'A good king is Charles. I'd drink his health … if I had a drink.'

The reporter smiled and signalled for the landlord to refill the old keeper's mug. After they had drunk the health of King Charles, Talbot Edwards sighed. 'So Tom Blood is dead, you say?'

The reporter nodded. 'I'm writing his story now. You know he'd just lost a court case to the Duke of Buckingham? The court ordered Blood to pay £10,000 to the duke. He was ruined.'

The old man looked up. 'So Colonel Blood came to a bad end after all,' he said.

The young woman spoke in a low voice so no one could overhear. 'There were stories that Blood had faked his death. That there was some other person's body in the coffin. The magistrates had it dug up and identified. It was Blood all right.'

Talbot Edwards looked disappointed. 'Trust Colonel Blood to cheat his enemies to the last.'

'Oh, but he didn't cheat them…' the woman began.

The old man cut in. 'He did, you know. Because he cheated them out of what they wanted most of all … what they really wanted was to see him hang!'

And in the smoky light of the tavern candles the old man chuckled so loud and long he could scarcely drink his ale.

Did you know ?

1 Colonel Blood was involved in many outrageous crimes in his lifetime. In 1660 he tried to capture Dublin Castle and hold its governor to ransom. When he failed he fled to Holland.

OH WELL BLOOD, WE'D NEVER HAVE GOT IT INTO A SACK ANYHOW

2 In 1661 one of Blood's partners in the Dublin Castle kidnap was taken to London for execution. Blood returned to England, overcame a guard of eight soldiers and rescued his friend.

3 Blood's greatest enemy was Lord Ormonde. One night Ormonde was on his way to a banquet when his coach was stopped by a band of armed men. They could have killed him on the spot but Blood wanted a more dramatic death for his enemy. He wanted him taken to Tyburn gallows and hanged like a common criminal. The coachman raised the alarm and the plot failed.

4 When Charles met Blood, the Colonel had the cheek to tell the king that the Crown Jewels weren't really worth that much. People said they were worth £100,000 – Blood said he wouldn't give £6,000 for them. Charles was amused and released the thief.

5 Not only did Blood get an Irish estate from Charles, he was also welcomed into the royal court where he was a popular figure. He was admired as the man who almost stole the Crown Jewels … and Talbot Edwards was almost as famous as the man who almost lost them.

The teacher and the lord

Who would you rather marry, a lord or a teacher?

PERSONALLY I'D RATHER MARRY A *CHIMPANZEE* THAN A TEACHER

In 1709 a Scottish woman had the choice between Robert Lord Balfour of Burleigh and a teacher, Henry Stenhouse.

SHE CHOSE LORD BALFOUR OF COURSE

She chose the *teacher*. Lord Balfour was furious. He decided to sort Henry the teacher out. He killed him. Lord Balfour was arrested.

CRUELTY TO ANIMALS I SUPPOSE

Arrested for *murder*, found guilty and sentenced.

KILLING A TEACHER? DESERVES AN HOUR'S DETENTION AT THE MOST

Lord Balfour was sentenced to *death*. He was thrown into prison and waited to be executed. When the warders came to lead him to the scaffold they found he'd gone. Lord Balfour had swapped clothes with his sister when she came to visit. He walked free. Of course the poor woman married neither of the men.

SAD. STILL IT COULD HAVE BEEN WORSE... SHE COULD HAVE MARRIED THE TEACHER!

Before Stuart times lords expected to get away with murder. James I put an end to that when he ordered the execution of Lord Maxwell for murder in 1613. Maxwell had called a peace conference with his ancient enemy, John Johnstone. When Johnstone arrived at the meeting place, Maxwell shot him. Maxwell expected James to pardon him because he was a lord. James didn't. Maxwell was beheaded … and the other lords were a bit more careful about who they murdered in future.

The Archbishop of Canterbury, on the other hand, *did* get away with murder. He was out hunting for deer when he carelessly shot one of his gamekeepers with a crossbow. King James I was told of the tragedy. 'Ah, well,' the king sighed, 'No one but a fool or a villain could blame the Archbishop. It could happen to anyone.' The Archbishop went free.

Painful punishments

1 Sir Walter Raleigh had been a hero in the days of old Queen Elizabeth. But he'd been accused of plotting against James I and was sentenced to death on the scaffold in 1603. James decided not to execute Raleigh – he thought he'd just lock him up instead. But James had to have his little joke. First he let Raleigh grovel for his life, then he let Raleigh climb on to the scaffold. The crowd held its breath and looked forward to a bit of blood splashing around. Only *then* did James let him know his life was spared.

After 13 years in jail he was released to seek gold in America. But Raleigh had upset the Spanish king, who demanded that James should execute him. James didn't have a very good reason to execute the old man – so he dug up the old 'plot' accusation from 1603. In 1618 Raleigh's head rested on the block for a second time. If he thought James was going to have another little joke he was disappointed. This time – 15 years after he'd first put his head on the block – it hit the ground.

2 The Duke of Monmouth led a rebellion against James II in 1685 but was defeated and captured. On the scaffold he tested the edge of the axe and said he thought it was a little blunt. The Duke offered the executioner, Jack Ketch, six gold guineas to do a quick, clean job. But the Duke was cooler than Ketch, who took about five chops to get the head off. The crowd was furious and Ketch had to be protected from them as he left.

3 They didn't have that problem in Halifax. They had a machine there to execute people. It was a guillotine. The blade was released by pulling on a rope. That rope was

passed to the crowd so everyone pulled together. That way no single person was to blame for the criminal's death. If the criminal had stolen an animal then it was tied to the rope and driven away. So a cow could guillotine a man!

4 A Scottish law said that people could be sentenced to drowning in the sea if they refused to support the Scottish church. No one believed the old law would ever be used again. But it was, in 1685. Sixty-year-old Margaret McLauchlan and 18-year-old Margaret Wilson were tied to stakes at low tide. As the tide rose the sea would drown them. The old woman was placed lower in the water. The officers hoped

she would die first and the sight would persuade young Margaret to change her religion. It didn't. Old Margaret drowned and a soldier put young Margaret out of her misery by forcing her head under the water.

5 Scotland wasn't a healthy place to be at that time. In 1691 the Scots chiefs were told to take an oath to show they were loyal to King William III. But they had to take that oath before January 1st 1692. Alisdair McIain, head of the Macdonald clan, went to Fort William to take the oath. He was told to go to Inverary, 60 miles away. He battled through snow storms and arrived six days too late.

That was enough for the Scottish secretary to order the killing of all the Macdonalds. Thirty-five men and an unknown number of women and children died when the commander of the Argyll regiment, Robert Campbell, ordered his men to massacre the defenceless Macdonalds in their village at Glencoe. To this day the Macdonalds and the Campbells are said to distrust each other.

6 The Puritans brought in new laws after they had won the Civil War. Puritan punishments included:

CRIME	PURITAN PUNISHMENT
A man disagreed with the Puritan religion	Soldiers sold his furniture sent his servants to London and dug up every tree in his orchard
A woman swore [seven rude words]	Fined 12 shillings [60°]
A barber trimmed someone's beard on a Sunday	Fined
A man stole lead from a house roof	Whipped for two hours 'till his body be bloody' and sent to prison till a fine was paid
Being actors in a travelling theatre company	Whipped and sat in stocks
A maid mended a dress on Sunday	Sat in the stocks for three hours
People went to church on Christmas Day	Sent to prison

The poet Richard Brathwaite wrote…

> *One day to Banbury I came*
> *And there I saw a Puritane*
> *Hanging of his cat on Monday*
> *Cos it killed a mouse on Sunday*

(Mr Brathwaite wrote that in 1638, of course. He wouldn't have dared to write that 12 years later when the Puritans were running the country!)

No wonder the people were pleased to see Charles II return. He really seemed to be a 'Merry Monarch' – but after the Puritan reign, a game of chess with a chimpanzee would have seemed a 'merry' idea.

7 An actor called Wilson played the part of 'Bottom' in Shakespeare's *Midsummer Night's Dream*. He had to dress as an ass for part of the play. The magistrates must have had a sense of humour. While Wilson sat in the stocks he wore a label round his neck saying .

> *Good people, I have played the beast,*
> *And brought bad things to pass.*
> *I was a man, but now I've made*
> *Myself a silly ass!*

I DON'T KNOW WHAT'S WORSE, THE STOCKS OR THE POETRY

8 A man called Titus Oates was sentenced to be tied to the back of a cart as it was driven from Aldgate to Newgate. As he was dragged along he was whipped. King James ordered that the treatment should be repeated on a second day. Oates was too weak to walk – he was fastened face down on a stretcher and dragged through the streets again being whipped. And Oates was lucky … he deserved worse! His crime was that he had dreamed up a story about a Catholic plot to murder Charles II. The country was thrown into a panic and innocent Catholics were tortured, executed or driven out of their homes by frightened Protestants. Oates claimed the Catholics had invited a French army to invade, and…

- An army was reported to have landed one night in Dorset – but in daylight the French soldiers turned out to be a hedge and their officers a few grazing horses.
- Chains were thrown across London streets to stop French cavalry charging.
- Tailors started selling 'armour' to rich men and women. It became very fashionable because it was silk armour.

WILL IT STOP A DAGGER?

CERTAINLY MADAM

IF IT'S A SILK DAGGER

9 William Prynne was a Member of Parliament and simply hated the theatre. He wrote a strong attack on plays and actors. Charles I on the other hand loved the theatre. So Charles had Prynne punished for his writing. Prynne had both ears cut off.

Five years later Prynne was writing nasty things about bishops. This time a judge said...

...*and* he pointed to a pair of stubs. These were cut off and he was branded on the cheeks.

William Prynne lived to see Charles II come to the throne – and Charles gave him a well-paid job in the Tower of London.

10 The dreadful Judge Jeffreys was especially thoughtful at Christmas time. He once sentenced a woman to be whipped but kindly added an instruction to the man with the whip, 'Pay particular attention to this lady. Beat her soundly till the blood runs down. It is Christmas, a cold time for madam to strip. See that you "warm" her shoulders thoroughly.'

11 When the Roundheads captured a Scottish Cavalier they put him in the stocks. They then held his mouth open with two sticks, pulled his tongue out to its full length and tied two sticks to it. The man couldn't pull his tongue back in. He had to stay like that for half an hour.

12 Not many people know that James I was a detective. True! A servant called Sarah Swarton said she had witnessed Lord Roos taking part in some hanky-panky with a woman who wasn't his wife. She said she'd hidden behind a window curtain in his Wimbledon home. Lady Roos went to King James to complain and have her husband punished. 'Sherlock' James went to the scene of the crime and asked the maid Sarah to stand behind the curtains. The curtains only came to her knees. She couldn't have stood there without being seen! Lord Roos was cleared – false-witness Sarah was charged with 'perjury', or lying after swearing to tell the truth. She was punished by being whipped then branded – she would probably have had the letter 'P' for perjurer burned into her cheek.

Potted punishments

Can you match the name of the Stuart punishment to its description?

NAME	DESCRIPTION *The victim...*
Branks	1. had his thumbs placed in a vice which was tightened until he talked
Repentance stool	2. was placed in a barrel with a hole in the top and bottom [For head and legs] and a hole in each side for the arms. Victim walked round street dressed in barrel
Cropping	3. had to wear an iron mask with a spike that went into the mouth. She then walked around the town wearing it. A punishment for women who nagged or talked too much

| Drunkard's cloak | 4. sits down in church while the priest tells everyone what a disgusting person this is |
| Thumbekins | 5. had his head put in a pillory and his ears nailed to the wood. The ears were then cut off and often left fastened to the pillory |

William (reigned 1689-1702) and Mary (reigned 1689-1694)

Slimy Mary

Mary had no regrets about taking the throne from her own father, James II, when he ran away to France. In fact, when she arrived at her father's palace, she was so happy she ran through the bedrooms and bounced on all the beds. (Mary was a large woman – but there is no record of the damage to the beds)

Slimy William

William had a girlfriend called Betty Villiers. Mary's father, James II, tried to stir up trouble between the couple. He said his spies had found out all about Betty Villiers – what was she going to do about it?

What she decided to do was have a very sharp word with William. But Willy used weasel words to worm his way out of it. 'I swear to you by all that is most sacred that I've done nothing wrong!' he lied.

Mary, the mug, believed him.

William sacked the spying servants ... and went on seeing Betty Villiers.

Dreadful deaths

Mary died in 1694 from smallpox. She was only 32 years old.

William died eight years later after falling off his horse. The horse stumbled on a mole hill.

He broke his collar bone and his surgeon 'set' it. He'd probably have recovered but he stupidly chose to return to Kensington Palace that evening. The coach ride was long and the Stuart roads rough. The broken bone was jerked out of place. This time it didn't heal and an infection eventually killed him. He died despite some incredible medicines … like powdered crabs' eyes!

The supporters of James II (who wanted the old king back) were thrilled. Over the years they drank many toasts to the mole that dug that hole.

Slimy Stuart facts

Are you a mastermind or a mug? Answer these questions *without cheating and looking at the answers first!* Score five or more and you're a Stuart Mastermind.

1 What souvenir could you buy at the coronation of Charles II?
a) A slice of coronation cake.
b) A coronation mug.
c) A piece of Charles's coronation robe.

2 Samuel Pepys wrote a famous diary in the middle of the Stuart period. What did he write with?
a) A fountain pen.
b) A typewriter.
c) The feather of a mongoose.

3 What would you do with a 'lobster tail pot'?
a) Eat it.
b) Go fishing with it.
c) Wear it.

4 How much would you expect to pay a well-trained maid in the middle of the 17th century?
a) Two pounds a year.
b) Twenty pounds a year.
c) A hundred pounds a year.

5 When Queen Henrietta first saw her baby Charles (later Charles II) what were her first words?
a) 'He looks just like his father.'
b) 'He is so beautiful I am quite, quite proud of him.'
c) 'He is so ugly I am ashamed of him.'

6 What was the London speed limit for coach drivers set in 1635?

a) Thirty miles an hour.

b) Three miles an hour.

c) Twelve miles an hour.

7 A well-known cure for measles was to go to bed with…

a) A warm drink of rum.

b) A warm brick.

c) A warm sheep.

8 At the siege of Basing House the Roundheads ran out of bullets. What did they do?

a) Made new ones from lead coffins dug up from the local graveyard.

b) Made new ones from lead off the church roof.

c) They picked up Cavalier bullets and fired them back.

9 Where would rich Stuart people get false teeth from?

a) Carpenters made wooden ones.

b) Potters made china ones.

c) Poor people sold their good ones.

10 The Stuarts had some strange names for their dance tunes. Which of these is NOT a Stuart dance tune?

a) *An Old Man's A Bed Full Of Bones*

b) *Punk s Delight*

c) *My Lady's a Wild Flying Dove*

Answers:

1 b) They were the first coronation souvenirs sold in Britain.

2 a) The fountain-pen didn't work too well and most people stuck with the old quill pen for another 200 years, but Pepys did use one of the first fountain pens from time to time.

3 c) The lobster pot was the name given to the Roundheads' helmets because of their curious shape. The neck guard was like a lobster's tail.

FLAP FLAP

4 a) A manservant would earn double what a maid could earn. A steward (the head servant) who ran a large house for its owner would expect £20 and the Earl of Bedford paid his steward the huge sum of £40 a year.

YE GODS BEDFORD, THAT'S OVER THREE POUNDS A MONTH!

WHAT IF EVERYONE WANTED THAT MUCH?

YOU'LL RUIN US!

5 c) Later, Charles grew up to agree with her. 'Odds fish, I am an ugly fellow,' he claimed. He said it!

6 b) Of course there were no policemen with speed traps – but if a coach overtook a walking law-officer he could face a fine.

7 c) 'Sheep', Stuart doctors said, 'are easily infected with measles and draw the sickness to themselves, by which means some ease may happen to the sick person.'

8 a) They scattered a lot of bones around but thoughtfully chalked the names of the dead on the wall so they would not be forgotten.

9 c) 'If a gentleman has lost his teeth there are dentists who will insert into his gums teeth pulled from the jaws of poor youths.' – *Advert*, 1660

10 c) This is a 1960's pop song. A 'punk' in Stuart times was a wild woman. a) and b) are genuine Stuart dance tunes and other titles included *Petticoat Wag* and *Dusty my dear*. Scotland had the delightful, *The Lamb's Wind*.

Stuart women and children

Women have had a pretty hard time in many eras of history. But some modern historians believe that Stuart women weren't too badly off – compared to the Tudor women who lived before them or the Georgians who came after them. Stuart women had the usual problems of staying beautiful, of course…

Ten beastly ways to beauty

Stuart Superwoman April 1664

Beauty Tips
PAGE

editor

Girls! Do *you* want to look special for that man in your life? Here are the top ten tips from our Beauty Editor, Patricia Pasteface.

I Hair flair – want to have those lovely locks glowing like gold? Then why not try washing them in rhubarb juice and white wine? If you prefer to be a red-head then dye it with radish and leaves from a privet hedge.

2 Silky skin – don't let spots spoil that special date. If you have spots then why not try rubbing in the blood of: a freshly killed cockerel or a pigeon? (But, girls, don't forget to wash the blood off before you leave the house!)

3 Pale complexion – we know men love that pale and interesting look. If you have a weather-beaten face then burn the jaw bone of a pig and grind it to a powder. Mix with poppy oil and rub it into the skin. It'll turn as pale and pink as that pig in no time. Of course every woman wears chicken-skin gloves at night to keep those fair hands soft and white.

4 Sparkling eyes – spread a cloth on the grass on any night in the month of May. In the morning it will be soaked with dew. Wring out the dew and collect it in bottles. A quick rinse will make sore red eyes as good as new. But remember, only *May* dew will do.

5 Body beautiful – soak for two or three hours in a bath that's waist deep. Fill the bath with three gallons of milk then stir in a boiled mixture of violet petals, rosemary, fennel, mallow and nettles. Step out of the bath then go to bed and sweat, being careful not to catch a cold.

6 Farewell to foul freckles – wash those ugly freckles away with water of strawberries or the juice from watercress.

7 Dental delight – take the herb rosemary and the alum flower and burn them. Clean your teeth with the ashes for that sweet, sweet smile. And remember … sleeping with your mouth open helps keep teeth white.

8 Rout the wrinkles – if your face has more creases than a cockerel's crest then wash them away with a mixture of elder flowers, irises, mallows and bean blossom.

9 In tune with the moon – wash your face in the weeks when the moon is growing smaller. Use a sponge morning and night in those two weeks and your beauty's guaranteed.

10 Teen queen – stay looking like a 15-year-old by washing in a mixture of eggs, asses milk and cinnamon spice.

These sound pretty useless treatments – but at least they were *harmless*. That's more than could be said for the gruesome Elizabethan make-up of a hundred years before. This had involved rubbing poisonous lead mixtures into the skin. And cleaning your teeth with ashes doesn't sound too tasty, but Stuart teeth were healthier than in most ages.

Of course, women were not only told they should be beautiful: they were also told how they should behave. You will notice that, as usual, it is a man who is telling them…

The English Housewife by Gevase Markham

THE NOTABLE HOUSEWIFE MUST…
- be brave
- be patient
- be tireless
  WAAA!
- speak wisely…
  A STITCH IN TIME SAVES NINE
- …but not too much
  mmmmf
- be secret in her affairs
  —DON'T SAY I TOLD YOU THIS BUT…

Witches

As in most other ages, most of the people accused of being witches in Stuart times were women. King James I was fascinated by witches. He believed there were several black-magic plots to kill him before he came to the English throne. He even wrote a book about witchcraft.

But the English were never quite as harsh towards witches as the Scots. A horrible history story from Victorian times could well be true...

The Witch of Irongray

'In the reign of James I, or in the early years of his son Charles's reign, there is a tale of a woman burned as a witch in the parish of Irongray in Scotland. In a little mud-walled cottage lived a poor woman who earned a little money by spinning wool and weaving stockings. She lived alone and was often seen on a summer's evening, sitting on a jagged rock above the Routing Stream.

Sometimes she would gather sticks, late on a November evening, among the rowan tree roots. Lying in her window she sometimes had a black-letter bible which had two brass clasps of a grotesque design to fasten it closed. When she went to church her lips were sometimes seen to be moving. She was known to forecast showers or sunshine at certain times and her forecasts were often right.

The Bishop of Galloway was urged to punish this woman for being a witch. He was afraid he'd be reported to the king if he failed to deal with her so he ordered her to be brought before him near to the Routing Stream.

She was dragged roughly from her home. Several neighbours were called to declare the wicked things that she had done.

She was sentenced to be drowned in the Routing Stream. But the crowd insisted that she should be shut up in a tar barrel and thrown into the River Cluden. Unwillingly the bishop agreed. The wretched woman was enclosed in a barrel, fire was set to it and it was rolled in a blaze into the waters of the Cluden.'

The unlucky woman was Alice Mulholland. The English gave up hanging witches during the reign of James II and they didn't have any more witch trials after 1712. But the Scots went on persecuting witches a little longer. The last to be burned for witchcraft in Scotland was in 1722.

Women were still 'ducked' on a stool into freezing water if they nagged too much. That nasty habit went on until 1817 when Sarah Leeke was ducked. It all ended as a bit of a joke – when Sarah Leeke was ducked they couldn't get her under the water. The pool they'd chosen was too shallow!

Cheerless children

Would you like to have been a child in Stuart times? If you were the child of a strict Puritan then you could have started off life badly by being stuck with a rotten religious name. Which of the following nasty names were really given to nippers?

1. SILENCE
2. HELPLESS
3. FORSAKEN
4. MISERICORDIA
5. FIGHT-THE-GOOD-FIGHT-OF-FAITH
6. SORRY-FOR-SIN
7. GOOD-FOR-NOTHING
8. POSTHUMA
9. LAMENT
10. DISCIPLINE

Answer: All except number 7 were Stuart christening names.

The Puritans also had:
Kill-sin, Increase, Faint-not, Desire, Search-the-scriptures, Remember, Seek-wisdom, If-Christ-had-not-died-thou-hadst-been-damned, Safety on-high.

There was also a name for those of us who have normal names – it was 'Be-thankful'!

Of course, you had to survive the christening ceremony in church. Stuart superstition said it was a good sign if the baby cried at its christening. That was a sign that the evil spirits were leaving it. Just to be on the safe side, the godparent holding the baby would give it a sharp nip to make it howl.

Toothy trouble
If you survived your christening then you still had to survive growing up. Many babies died because Stuart families didn't understand about germs. For every 100 people who died in Stuart times, 40 were under two years old.

Some rich parents couldn't be bothered with wailing and whingeing babies. They sent the baby away to nurses in the country until the child was old enough to walk and talk. They visited it from time to time.

Of course when a baby starts to cut its teeth it tends to cry a lot. The nurses had an answer. In *The Queen's Chest*, published in 1664, there was a little recipe for soothing those painful gums…

Boil the head of a hare. Mix the brains with honey and butter. Rub the mixture on the gums as often as you please.

Boil the head of a hare. Mix the brains with honey and butter. Rub the mixture on the gums as often as you please

Switching schools

Would you like a school switch? Probably *not* if it was a Stuart school switch. Because a switch was a thin wooden stick and it was used to beat naughty boys … girls didn't usually go to school.

Some people thought boys should have this thin 'switch' rather than the stiff wooden 'ferula'…

As for the ferula I wish it could be banned from schools. A good birch switch will not break bones or damage limbs. A good switch about the shoulders should be sufficient.

(Charles Hoole 1660)

Isn't that kind?

The rules of Chigwell school suggested…

Schoolmasters should not give more than three strokes of the rod at any one time. They should not strike any scholar upon the head or the cheek with their fist. They should not curse or swear at the pupils.

At least the Stuart pupils had one day every year when they could get their own back. Teachers handed power over to the pupils for a day and the pupils could use it to lock out the teacher – this was called 'Barring out'. Would you like to suggest it to your teachers? But there had to be rules, of course…

- The school master must know about it beforehand.
- The pupils must behave politely.
- Pupils must not use weapons to injure one another.
- Pupils must not damage the school.

Doesn't sound so much fun now, does it? In fact 'Barring-out day' sometimes got out of hand. In a Birmingham school in 1667 the governors complained…

Some of the scholars, being assisted by certain townsmen, did put into practice a violent exclusion of their master from the school. Though they deserted the school at about nine o'clock at night on the 27th November, some returned on 28th with unruly members of the town wearing masks and carrying pistols. Then they not only threatened to kill their school master but, for two hours, tried to break in. They threw stones and bricks at him through the window and broke through the walls of the school to endanger his life.

That sounds a bit more lively, doesn't it? The report went on to say…

Some governors think the master should pardon the offending scholars. But they believe the people from the town who joined the riot should be punished by the law. Any pupil who attempts to exclude the master again should be expelled.

So now you know. Getting the town toughs to attack your teacher is *not allowed*. Not even if teacher's a bit of a crook like the ones at Caistor School in 1631 where the school was *supposed* to be free and…

> *The schoolmasters are not to expect, demand or extract money for teaching any child, other than their wage.*

But they did. The rich parents paid the school teacher *extra* money to give their children *extra* lessons. (Of course, nowadays your teachers are so well paid they wouldn't dream of taking extra money from your parents, would they?)

In 1673 Bathusa Makin opened a school for young ladies. She wrote that there would be more schools like hers but they wouldn't be popular with men. 'I expect to meet with many scoffs,' she said, 'because men would be ashamed of their ignorance.' In other words, brainy girls would show the boys up. (She could be right.)

Joyless jobs
Stuart boys would often be sent to learn a trade as an *apprentice* as soon as they left school. Their father would pay a skilled craftsman to teach his son a trade.

This was like another five to eight years of school … only *worse* in some cases. A boy called Francis was sent to a scrivener for eight years to learn how to be a clerk. After three years he was suffering so much he wrote home to his father to complain. The letter may have gone something like this…

January 1643

Dear Dad

That's it I want to come home. Three years I've suffered here with old Bootley and I've had enough. There are three apprentices here and one of them is Bootley's own son. So guess who gets all the rotten jobs? That's right. Me

It's bad enough getting the boring copying to do. But you didn't tell me I'd have to slave in the house as well! Who cleans the boots before breakfast? Me. And who empties the ashes, fills the coal bucket, sweeps the shop, and cleans that nasty long sink? Me. I'm supposed to be learning to be a clerk!

Then Mrs Bootley uses me like a manservant. I'm in the middle of writing and what happens? The kitchen maid comes and orders me to fetch Mrs Bootley a farthing's worth of mustard or a pint of vinegar. Last week she sent me for a pint of beer, didn't like the taste, and sent me back to change it.

You paid old Boot-face thirty pounds for this. AND you paid him a hundred pounds for my good behaviour. If I make trouble you lose that hundred pounds. I know. So I daren't make a fuss. Just take me away from here! Your loving son

Frances

What happened to Francis after the letter was sent?

1 Francis's father complained to Mr Bootley and things got better.

2 Francis's father complained to Mr Bootley and Mr Bootley beat Francis with a cane…

3 Francis's father took his son away from Mr Bootley and lost his £130.

Many masters *deliberately* treated their apprentices badly. They took a dozen apprentices at £50 each and made them so miserable that they ran away. The parents couldn't get the money back and the masters were hundreds of pounds richer.

Awful apprentices

The teenage apprentices often went around in gangs and were the 'problem' kids of their time. When the Puritans abolished holidays it was the London apprentices who went on strike to get them back.

In Tudor Newcastle there had been laws to stop them 'playing dice and cards, drinking, dancing and embracing 'women'. The older people thought the apprentices looked disgraceful with their silk-lined clothes, bearded faces and daggers at their belts: 'They are more like raging ruffians than decent apprentices.'

Fifty years later when James I came to the throne, nothing much had changed – except the apprentices had to find new ways to make trouble, and the old fogies had to find new ways to stop them.

A 1603 law said, 'Apprentices are forbidden to use any music by night or day in the streets. Nor shall they wear their hair long over their ears.'

Young people of today argue with their parents and their teachers about hair styles – perhaps you do! Then just be glad you didn't live in 17th-century Newcastle. Anyone found guilty of having long hair was…

• Sentenced to jail…
• *And* to having a basin put over the head and the hair chopped off along the edges!

University students had the same problem. In 1636 Edmund Verney went for his final exam with the head of his college. He wrote home to Dad, 'The head spoke to me very politely as he could not find fault with my hair, because I had cut it before I went to him.'

Battered bride

There was some sort of equality for women in Stuart times. Boys were beaten with sticks … girls were beaten too!

Young Frances Coke didn't want to marry the rich John Villiers. John had occasional fits of madness when he might smash a glass in his hand and bleed all over the floor. Maybe Frances didn't fancy mopping up after him.

Her Father, Sir Edward Coke, said she *had* to marry John Villiers. There were 10,000 good reasons why she should – John was paying Sir Edward £10,000 for Frances's hand.

£10,000 FOR MY HAND? I WONDER WHAT THE REST OF ME IS WORTH?

Frances ran away with her mother and hid. Sir Edward found the house, battered down the door and dragged the girl from the cupboard where she was hiding.

'Marry John Villiers or else,' she was told.

'No,' she replied.

So she got the 'or else'. She was 'tied to the bedposts and whipped.'

She changed her mind – wouldn't you? – and finally agreed to marry the loathsome John Villiers.

Frances Coke was just fourteen years old at the time. Frances and John did not make a happy couple. She found a new boyfriend and ran off to live with him.

But it wasn't a happy ending. She lost her fortune to John Villiers's grasping family and she died in poverty.

Talk like a Stuart

Every age has its own slang. Are any of your schoolmates 'bagpipes' or 'barnacles?' (That's chatter boxes or hangers-on, of course.)

Do you have any 'muck in the sack of your kicks' at the moment? (That's money in the pocket of your trousers, if you hadn't guessed.)

Slimy Stuart villains

A book called *Leathermore s Advice* was published in 1666 and the writer complained…

Towards night there come Hectors, Trepanners, Guilts, Pads, Biters, Prigs, Divers, Lifters, Kid-Nappers, Vouchers, Mill-kens, Pymen, Decoys, Shop-lifters, Foilers, Bulkers, Droppers, Famblers, Dannakers, Crosbyters… generally known as Rooks.

You might not understand what he was writing about, but you get the picture. Stuart towns were not a safe place to be at night.

Why not amaze and impress your teacher/parent/gerbil by reciting this sad tale. They will certainly say, 'Well!/ Gosh!/Eeeek!' … and then ask you to explain.

The fate of the fustilugs

There once was a fustilugs[1] slabberdegullion[2]
Who grew up quite buffle[3], not dossy[4].
He learned how to mill-ben[5], to pug[6] and to dub[7]
Then this dunaker[8] jiggled[9] a hossy[10].

But at budging[11] a beak[12] he was such a fopdoodle[13]
He was caught and sent down to the clink[14].
'Oh the cage[15] belly-timber[16] is pannam[17] and old horse[18]
And we only get water to drink.'

1 a dirty eared child
2 a slob
3 stupid
4 brainy
5 break and enter houses
6 steal
7 pick locks
8 animal thief
9 rustled
10 horse – all right, this is *not* a Stuart slang word – but *you* try finding something to rhyme with 'dossy'
11 dodging
12 constable – later a judge
13 useless person
14 the name of a London prison
15 prison
16 food
17 bread
18 dried, salted beef

Beware the bung-napper![1]

If you wanted to survive in Stuart Britain you had to know who was out to get you. Can you match the criminals to their methods and their crimes?

THIS CRIMINAL	WOULD...	AND...
DARKMAN'S BUDGE	WAIT BY THE ROADSIDE	STEAL FROM YOUR HOUSE
SNOWDROPPER	HIDE IN YOUR HOUSE TILL DARK	ROB STAGE COACHES
SNUDGE	PLAY CARDS WITH YOU	LET A GANG INTO YOUR HOUSE
THIMBLE-RIGGER	CLIMB INTO YOUR HOUSE	STEAL YOUR WASHING
FOOTPAD	WALK PAST YOUR HEDGE	CHEAT YOU OUT OF MONEY

1 purse-snatcher

109

And that's not all! A *sneaksman* was the lowest sort of thief. He just sort of lurked around and pinched anything he could get his hands on. A bit like next-door's cat.

- A *foist* would dip his hand into your pocket or purse while a *nip* would use a knife to cut a purse that hung from your belt. We'd call them pickpockets today.

- A *leatherhead* or a *ding boy* would simply beat you up and take your money – a bit like the school bully. (Note: It is *not* a good idea to call the school bully either of these names!)

- A *varnisher* would give you a fake coin – smartened up with (guess what?) a coat of varnish.

- Nothing was safe! Because you may find a *buffernapper* has pinched your dog or a *bleating cull* might snaffle your sheep. (Would we call him a *ram raider* today?)

Aren't you just glad you live in the 20th century where all you have to worry about are hackers (who don't use a hacksaw), twockers (who don't steal twocks), muggers (who aren't after your mug), armed robbers (who have three arms … left-arm, right-arm and fire-arm) and serial killers…

Fox your friends

Say these two sentences to a friend then ask which of the two makes sense:

1. I'M NOT PLAYING MONOPOLY WITH YOU BECAUSE YOU USE A BRISTLE

2. DID YOU KNOW THE RIVER AVON RUNS THROUGH THE TOWN OF BRISTLE?

Answer: 1 A bristle was a dice that was 'loaded' to show any number the thrower wanted. It was used by slimy Stuart cheats.

Stuart fun and games

Fun at the fair

Stuart fairs were great holiday events. Lots of food … and fighting. Lots of weird and wonderful entertainments. Can you picture this rope dancer from the description in the *Daily Courant* newspaper?

the Daily Courant

DANCERS ON A ROPE

At the Great Booth will be seen the famous company of rope dancers, the greatest performers of dancing on the low-rope, and walking on the slack and sloping rope. They are said to be the only amazing wonders in the world in every thing they do.

There you will see the Italian Scarramouch dancing on a rope. He has a wheel-barrow in front of him with two children and a dog in it. He also has a duck on his head who sings to the crowd and causes much laughter.

John Evelyn described a fire eater in his diary…

> *He devoured glowing coals before us, chewing and swallowing them. He melted a beer glass and ate it quite up. Then he take a live coal on his tongue and put on it a raw oyster. The coal was blown with bellows until it flamed and sparkled in his mouth. There it remained until the oyster was quite boiled. Then he melted tar and wax which he drank down as it flamed; I saw it flaming in his mouth a good while.*

Slimy toads

If you lived in Stuart times you'd probably look forward to the annual fair in your area. Just like today's fairs there was magic, excitement and danger . . . and special food.

But would you like to eat a slithery, slimy *live* toad? Probably not. What about if someone offered you money to swallow that toad? Probably not. Because, not only would it be disgusting, it would probably kill you.

So one of the strangest sights at a Stuart fair would be the Mountebank. (A Mountebank was a man who called himself a doctor.) Imagine him going through the fair selling miracle cures…

'Ladies and gentlemen,' the Mountebank cries. 'Do you ever suffer from problems of digestion and distempers? Why suffer when you can try Doctor Cureall's Herbal Healing Tonic? This tonic is made from herbs to a secret and ancient recipe from ancient Egypt. It includes such rare ingredients as powdered mummy from an Egyptian pharaoh.'

'Rubbish!' someone calls from the crowd around him.

'Ah! We have a disbeliever, do we? Well, sir, what must I do to prove my miracle cure? I'll tell you what I'll do … I'll poison someone, then cure them!' the Mountebank smiles. He reaches into his black bag and pulls out a fat, warty toad. 'I have here a toad. Probably the most poisonous creature known to mankind. If anyone swallowed this then it would lead to almost certain death, would it not?'

There is a muttering amongst the crowd. They agree toads are poisonous.

'My miracle cure will defeat even the might of a toad's powerful poison. Now, can I have a volunteer to swallow this toad? Some brave person?' The Mountebank turns to the man who shouted 'Rubbish!' and offers it to him. The man turns his head away in disgust.

'Very well, I shall pay someone *six pence* if they will offer to swallow this deadly creature then be revived by my potion. No one? *Ten* pence, anyone? Very well I shall offer *one shilling* plus a free bottle of Doctor Cureall's Herbal Healing Tonic – which is worth a shilling itself. Do I have a volunteer?'

A shabby young man steps forward. 'I'll do it for a shilling,' he says.

'Ladies and gentlemen, a round of applause for this gallant young man.' The crowd claps. The noise of their clapping brings more fair visitors into the circle round the rough wooden stage. Everyone is hooked on this performance now.

Doctor Cureall pulls the stopper from a dark-blue bottle. I shall have the Herbal Healing Tonic ready to administer. But don't worry, young man, Doctor Cureall's tonic will work even if you are *dead!*'

The Mountebank passes the toad to the young man who looks at it nervously. 'One shilling,' Doctor Cureall promises, 'just for swallowing this creature.'

The scruffy young man closes his eyes, tilts back his head … and quickly pushes the toad into his gaping mouth. He gives a huge swallow. The crowd gasps, and waits.

The volunteer's face begins to crease in pain. He gives a low moan and clutches at his stomach. His eyes begin to pop with the strain. He falls to his knees and cries, 'The cure! The cure!'

The Mountebank holds the bottle in the air, well out of the reach of the cringing young man. 'Shall I give him the cure?'

Someone laughs nervously, 'Let him die. Serve him right!'

But the young man screams in agony. 'Give him the cure,' someone shouts. Others join in, 'For God's sake, give him the cure!'

By now the young man is lying on the stage, rolling in agony. Doctor Cureall slowly reaches down and forces the bottle between the lips of the dying man. He drinks it greedily. Slowly his twisting body calms and he lies still on the stage. The crowd is silent.

The young man opens one eye. Then the other eye. He raises his head from the stage. He looks at his stomach with wonder and sits up. 'It's a miracle!' he cries. 'Here, Doctor Cureall, don't give me a shilling... just give me another bottle of that Herbal Healing Tonic!' He jumps to his feet and clutches at his two free bottles as if they were liquid gold. The Mountebank turns to the crowd. 'Now, who else would like a bottle – only a shilling for a bottle of the secret of life itself'

The crowd pushes and jostles to force money into the happy Mountebank's hand.

It is the end of the busy fair. And it is dark behind the Mountebank's stage. The doctor is counting his money when a by young man approaches. 'Have you had a good day, Doc?'

'Eight pounds and 16 shillings, my toady-eating friend. And here are your five shillings for your excellent job.'

The young man jingles the coins happily in his hand and turns to find a tavern to spend them in.

'I think you've forgotten something,' the Mountebank says sharply.

The young man grins a yellow-toothed grin. He reaches into his pocket and hands something over to Doctor Cureall.

A fat, warty toad.

Toad-eating facts

1 No one is quite sure how toad-eaters managed the trick. The young toad eater was probably a clever magician who *appeared* to eat a toad but never did.

2 When a toad is attacked it squeezes out a deadly milky poison. If the smell doesn't put off the attacker then the taste will. A dog trying to eat a toad will start foaming at the mouth and howling.

3 Even the Romans knew about toad poison. There is a record of Roman women using toad poison to kill their husbands. They threw the toad into boiling water and the poison rose to the surface. It was skimmed off and fed to the unlucky man.

4 Italian poisoners of Stuart times had learned to blend toad poison with salt.

5 Toad-eating was considered to be the lowest form of job. Clowns and jugglers at the fairs were more respected than a toad-eater.

6 A real creep will do anything for their boss, no matter how disgusting. So in Stuart times a new word was invented for creeps – 'toad-eater'.

7 Later the word changed to 'toady'. So instead of calling a pupil a teacher's pet' they would be called a 'toady' in Stuart times.

8 Some people swore they saw the toady swallow the toad. So, was it possible? There is just a chance that toad eaters really did swallow live toads … and live. How? The toads could have been 'pets' who learned to trust their trainers. He might even allow them to sit on his tongue for a while so they didn't get excited by the idea and sweat poison. Then, on the day of the fair, he popped the happy toad on his tongue – and swallowed it quickly before the toad could react.

9 A young man who was fit, and who had just eaten a good meal, could probably survive a toad swallowing in this way. It could give him stomach and head pains, but he'd live.

10 A toady who wasn't fit could well die.

Next time someone offers you some sausage in a batter pudding, known as 'Toad in the Hole', you'll know what to say: 'Did I ever tell you about people who ate real toads…'

Eating toads wasn't the only fun you could have at a Stuart fair. There were prizes to win on the side shows and there were presents to take home for the family. Gifts to take home from the fair were known as 'fairings.' A popular fairing was a coloured ribbon.

There are many songs written about fairs. One of the most famous is 'O dear, what can the matter be?'

> *O dear, what can the matter be?*
> *Dear, dear, what can the matter be?*
> *O dear, what can the matter be?*
> *Johnny's so long at the fair.*

> *He promised to buy me a pair of sleeve buttons,*
> *A pair of new garters that cost him just tuppence,*
> *He promised he'd bring me a bunch of blue ribbons*
> *To tie up my bonny brown hair.*

But, did you know … young men would often go to the fair, drink too much beer and fall asleep. In the 1700s the navy 'Press Gang' would kidnap these sleeping young men and take them off to serve in the navy.

That could be why Johnny was so long at the fair … he'd been press-ganged!

120

Sick Stuart sport

The Tudors, like Henry VIII and Elizabeth I, were supposed to live in cruel times, while the Stuarts are often thought of as 'modern'. The terrible truth is the Stuarts could be just as vicious as the Tudors … or the Vikings for that matter! Here's a report from the end of the Stuart age. Make up your own mind about how 'modern' the Stuarts were from this report by a foreign visitor…

June 23, 1710

Towards evening we drove to see the bull-baiting, which is held here nearly every Monday in two places. On the morning of the day the bull, or any other creature that is to be baited is led round. It takes place in a large open space or courtyard, on two sides of which high benches have been made for the spectators. First a young ox or bull was led in and fastened by a long rope to an iron ring in the middle of the yard; then about thirty dogs, two or three at a time, were let loose on him but he made short work of them, goring them and tossing them high in the air about the height of the first storey. Then amid shouts and yells the butchers to whom the dogs belonged sprang forward and caught their beasts right side up to break their fall. They had to keep hold of the dogs to hinder them from returning to the attack without barking. Several had such a grip of the bull's throat or ear that their mouths had to be forced open with poles

When the bull had stood it tolerably long, they brought out a small bear and tied him up in the same fashion. As soon as the dogs had at him he stood up on his hind legs and gave some terrific buffets; but if one of them got at his skin he rolled about in such a fashion that the dogs thought themselves lucky if they came out safe from beneath him.

But the most diverting and worst of all was a common little ass, who was brought out saddled with an ape on his back. As soon as a couple of dogs had been let loose on him he broke into a prodigious gallop – for he was free, not having been tied up like the other beasts – and he stamped and bit all around himself. The ape began to scream most terribly for fear of falling off. If the dogs came too near him, he seized them with his mouth and twirled them round shaking them so much that they howled prodigiously. Finally another bull appeared, on whom several crackers had been hung; when these were lit and several dogs let loose on him on a sudden, there was a monstrous hurly-burly. And thus was concluded this truly English sport, which vastly delights this nation but to me seemed nothing very special   Zacharius von Uffenbach

In 1760 bull-baiting was finally banned in Newcastle-upon-Tyne. A young sailor was gored in an accident. The 'sport' was banned because it was dangerous to the public, not because it was cruel to the animals!

Anne (reigned 1702-1714)

Anne was shy, stout, short-sighted and suffered from gout. In fact her gout was so painful that she had to be carried to her coronation!

She had 17 babies and 16 died. Only William survived infancy ... then *he* died at the age of 11.

Slimiest act

Would you betray your dear old dad? Anne did. Anne was Protestant and didn't want to follow her Catholic father, James II, during the 'Glorious Revolution'.

She didn't *exactly* 'jump out of the window' but she *did* make a secret escape at night down the back stairs. James went into exile and never sat on the throne again ... but Anne got her (very) fat bum on the throne 14 years later.

The Spiteful Stuart

Anne died in 1714 – she had grown so fat that when she died her coffin was almost square. Anne was the last of the Stuarts. Some said she was the *best*.

Her *friends* and *family* didn't say that.
Among the people she was spiteful towards were…

• Best friend Sarah Churchill – she was sent away when it suited the queen. Sarah was in tears, pleading for another chance. All Anne could reply was, 'Put it in writing'.

• Loyal adviser Earl of Godolphin – he was sacked. Anne didn't even tell him to his face. She just sent a message for him to snap his symbol of authority (a white staff) and get out.
• Her great army commander, Marlborough, who had won brilliant battles for her – he was sacked with a letter so nasty that he threw it into the fire and never spoke of it again.

124

• Her step-brother, James – Anne was quick to spread the rumour that he wasn't really her father's son; he was just a baby smuggled into the birth room in a warming pan. She then did an about-turn and tried to get baby James the throne when she died, instead of…

• Her successor George I – she knew his family would come to the throne of Britain when she died but she banned any of them from entering the country while she lived. Her main reason was simply that she disliked George.

For over 100 years her family had battled with Parliament. Anne brought peace by attending the House of Lords in person. She sat on the throne and listened to the debates – or in winter sat on a bench by the fire. When she died her doctor said, 'She welcomed death like a weary traveller welcomes sleep.'

Some Members of Parliament couldn't believe the news. 'She's not dead!' they tried to argue.

'Dead!' came the reply. 'She's as dead as Julius Caesar. '

I WONDER WHAT SIZED COFFIN *HE* NEEDED?

Epilogue

Anne was as dead as Julius Caesar, but the Stuarts weren't quite as dead as a hedgehog squashed on the road. They kept trying to get that throne back. In the next 31 years the family of James II had a couple of attempts – 1715 and 1745 if you're really interested in dates.

A prince from Germany, George I, was invited to take over when Anne died. A new family sat on the throne the Hanovers. George I didn't speak English and never bothered to learn – he was especially cruel to his wife, whom he had locked up for 32 years.

The British people did not like George I. But they *didn't* support the Stuart attempts to get the throne back. Why not? Because they hated the slimy Stuarts *more* than the horrible Hanovers!

Kings had been overthrown (or over-throne) before in British history. They had been 'usurped' by powerful *lords*. But the Slimy Stuarts lost power to *the people*. And they didn't manage this once – they did it *twice*.

Now *that's* unpopularity for you. Quite simply, the Brits didn't want a Catholic monarch. The Stuarts kept *saying* they were Protestants – but acting like Catholics. That's sneaky and sly – slimy in fact.

Lots of innocent people died in civil war and revolutions during the reign of the Stuarts. Next time you light a firework on the fifth of November, look into the sparks and say to yourself...

> *Remember, remember the fifth of November,*
> *Gunpowder treason and plot.*
> *Was Guy Fawkes a devil, the Stuarts all saints?*
> *Are we glad that they stopped him . . . or not?*

SLIMY STUARTS

GRISLY QUIZ

Now find out if you're a
slimy Stuarts expert!

SUPERSTAR SHAKESPEARE

HONORIFICABILITUDINITATIBUS

William Shakespeare used 17,677 different words in his writing. Amazingly, about 1,700 of those were new words! Can you spot the words (or phrases) first used by Shakespeare?

1. A place to stay is...
a) accommodation
b) a hotel
c) hard to find

2. If you're puzzled you say...
a) it's Greek to me
b) I don't understand
c) eh, you what?

3. If you're not mean you're...
a) kind
b) generous
c) sharing your chocolate biscuits

4. If you're unashamed you're...
a) open
b) barefaced
c) a nudist

5. To make someone go faster say...
a) quicken
b) hurry
c) little puff

6. A sudden wind is a...
a) blast
b) gust
c) little puff

7. A children's game is...
a) leapfrog
b) hopscotch
c) hopfrog

8. A reliable person is a...
a) tower of strength
b) brick
c) teacher

9. A person with no friends is...
a) lonely
b) friendless
c) smelly

10. Something that gets smaller…

a) dwindles

b) lessens

c) goes like a jumper in a hot wash

11. An lethal attack on a powerful person is…

a) murder

b) assassination

c) a bad idea

REMEMBER, REMEMBER…

Since the Gunpowder Plot was discovered it has passed into English history and is remembered every 5 November. But how many of these funny Fawkes facts are false?

1. In January 1606 Parliament passed a new law. It said that 5 November would become a holiday of public thanksgiving.

2. Guy Fawkes hasn't always been the one on top of bonfires. At different times in history dummies of different people have been burned on 5 November.

3. It wasn't until 1920 that fireworks were added to the 5 November celebrations.

131

4. For many years the people of Scotton village in Yorkshire refused to celebrate 5 November with fireworks and bonfires.

5. The government decided that the cellars beneath Parliament should be patrolled night and day to prevent another Gunpowder Plot. That patrol stopped a long time ago.

QUICK QUESTIONS

1. At the Civil War battle of Edgehill the famous doctor, William Harvey, settled down with a book as soldiers fell all around him. When he grew cold he pulled what over his legs to keep warm? (Clue: the doctor was no use to them)

2. Charles I was captured by Oliver Cromwell's army and held prisoner in Newcastle. They let him out to play what game in the nearby fields? (Clue: join the club)

3. Charles I went to his execution in 1649 wearing two shirts. Why? (Clue: it was 30 January 1649)

4. Sir Arthur Aston had a wooden leg so he was easily caught in a 1649 Irish battle. He was beaten to death. With what? (Clue: did he put his foot in it?)

5. Oliver Cromwell died in 1658 and the public queued to see his mummified body. But it began to go rotten. What did the government do next? (Clue: you wooden believe it)

6. Charles's head was sewn back on so he'd look good in his coffin. But his tomb was entered many years later and the neck bone stolen. It was used at the dinner table by Henry Halford. For what? (Clue: needed on chops!)

7. In 1653 Charles Culpepper wrote that this plant clears bad chests, cures headaches, worms and indigestion, and the juice kills lice in children's hair. What is this wonder plant? (Clue: it cures nothing and has killed millions)

8. In 1660 Charles II returned and punished the men who had had his dad, Charles I, beheaded. One condemned man had his belly opened and his guts lifted out for burning. How did he shock his executioner? (Clue: you can't keep a good man down)

TEST YOUR TEACHER...

How much does your history teacher know about the 1600s? Test them with this quiz — and if they get more than half wrong, threaten them with the Stuart cure for consumption!

1. Why were Oliver Cromwell's followers called 'Roundheads'?
a) because of the shape of their helmets
b) it was an insulting name given to them by the Cavaliers
c) because of their haircuts

2. Which Stuart king was described as 'a nervous drivelling idiot'?
a) James I
b) Charles I
c) James II

3. How did Charles II describe himself?
a) 'the most handsome man in England'
b) 'the King of Elegance'
c) 'an ugly fellow'

4. Who was the leader of the Gunpowder plot?
a) Guy Fawkes
b) Robert Catesby
c) Simon Montfort

5. Prince Rupert, a Cavalier leader during the Civil War, had a dog he took with him everywhere. What breed was it?
a) a black Great Dane
b) an Irish Wolfhound
c) a white Poodle

6. When he was a prince escaping from England (because his father had lost the Civil War), James II dressed as
a) a girl
b) a servant
c) Little Red Riding Hood

7. In the 1600s, who were Stroller's Priests and what did they do?
a) tramps who performed illegal marriages for couples
b) priests who roamed the countryside doing good works
c) thieves who stole from churches

8. What was a 'bung-napper' in Stuart times?
a) a sleep-walker

b) a purse-snatcher

c) a dustman

9. Which of the following was a real 1600s cure for spots?

a) drinking vinegar mixed with chopped-up worms

b) washing in your own pee

c) rubbing in the blood of a freshly killed pigeon

10. Who did Londoners blame for starting the Great Fire of London in 1666?

a) French spies

b) Catholics

c) plague victims

Answers

Superstar Shakespeare

1.a) 2.a) 3.b) 4.b) 5.b) 6.b) 7.a) 8.a) 9.a) 10.a) 11.b)
Anyone who answered c) has a brain like Shakespeare's!
(Dead for 400 years.)

Remember, remember...

1. True. People lit bonfires to celebrate and threw dummies on the fire dressed as Guy Fawkes.
2. True. The first record of this was at Cliffe Hill in

London 1606 where a dummy of the Pope joined Guy Fawkes in the flames.

3. False. Within a few years of the plot people began to use fireworks on November 5.

4. True. This village was where Guy Fawkes used to live and the people didn't think it was fair that Guy should take all the blame.

5. False. A search of the cellars is still carried out before the opening of every Parliament.

Quick Questions

1. Corpses. He was used to cutting them up for experiments so he wasn't too bothered about using them as blankets.

2. Golf. A popular game with his family, and granny Mary Queen of Scots enjoyed it too.

3. Charles didn't want to shiver in the cold in case people thought he was shaking with fear.

4. With his own wooden leg.

5. They replaced the corpse with a painted wooden dummy with glass eyes.

6. As a salt cellar.

7. Tobacco. Culpepper even said tobacco ash was good for cleaning the teeth! Ugh!

8. He sat up and hit the man who was cutting him open! That took guts!

Test your teacher
1.c) 2.a) 3.c) 4.b) 5.c) 6.a) 7.a) 8.b) 9.c) 10.a)

INTERESTING INDEX

Where will you find 'bird-droppings', 'chamberpots',
'rhubarb-juice' and 'toad-eaters' in an index? In a
Horrible Histories book, of course!

Terry Deary was born at a very early age, so long ago he can't remember. But his mother, who was there at the time, says he was born in Sunderland, north-east England, in 1946 – so it's not true that he writes all *Horrible Histories* from memory. At school he was a horrible child only interested in playing football and giving teachers a hard time. His history lessons were so boring and so badly taught, that he learned to loathe the subject. *Horrible Histories* is his revenge.

Martin Brown was born in Melbourne, on the proper side of the world. Ever since he can remember he's been drawing. His dad used to bring back huge sheets of paper from work and Martin would fill them with doodles and little figures. Then, quite suddenly, with food and water, he grew up, moved to the UK and found work doing what he's always wanted to do: drawing doodles and little figures.

Make sure you've got the whole horrible lot!

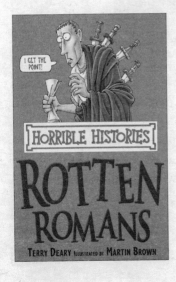

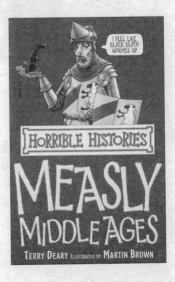